Stars on Stage

EILEEN DARBY & BROADWAY'S GOLDEN AGE

STARS ON

Stage

PHOTOGRAPHS 1940–1964

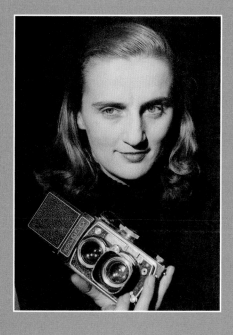

MARY C. HENDERSON

INTRODUCTION BY JOHN LAHR

BULFINCH PRESS   NEW YORK ~ BOSTON

BULFINCH PRESS

Time Warner Book Group
1271 Avenue of the Americas, New York, NY 10020
Visit our Web site at www.bulfinchpress.com

First Edition

PUBLISHED BY ARRANGEMENT WITH LTD EDITIONS

Library of Congress Cataloging-in-Publication Data
Darby, Eileen, 1916–2004.
    Stars on stage : Eileen Darby and Broadway's Golden Age : photographs 1940–1964 / [compiled by] Mary C. Henderson ; introduction by John Lahr. — 1st ed.
        p.   cm.
    Includes index.
    ISBN 0-8212-2897-8
    1. Stage photography — New York (State) — New York.   2. Actors — New York (State) — New York — Portraits.   3. Darby, Eileen, 1916–2004.
I. Henderson, Mary C.   II. Title.
TR817.D37   2005
779'.9792'097471 — dc22   2004022568

Art direction and book design by John Lynch

PAGE 1: Ethel Merman in *Annie Get Your Gun* (1946).

PAGE 2: Marlon Brando and Jessica Tandy in *A Streetcar Named Desire* (1947).

PAGE 3: Eileen Darby (circa 1942).

RIGHT: Gertrude Lawrence answering fan mail in her dressing room during the production of *Lady in the Dark* (1941).

PAGE 6: The crew of the show-within-a-show in *Me and Juliet* (1953).

PAGE 7: A production number from *Me and Juliet* (1953).

Printed in Singapore

IN LOVING MEMORY OF
JOHN AND LILLIAN BORQUEST DARBY
—*Eileen Darby Lester*

AND IN FOND MEMORY OF
EILEEN DARBY,
A GREAT PHOTOGRAPHER
AND AN EVEN GREATER WOMAN
—*Mary C. Henderson*

Acknowledgments

THIS BOOK could not have been published without the full cooperation of
Eileen Darby's family. Her daughter Virginia "Ginny" Teslik and her
grandson Alex Teslik were tireless in searching the files for that elusive
photograph and identification of plays and actors. Our gratitude to them is
boundless. Eileen's life-long friend Murray Garrett gave many interesting
insights into her career and provided a living portrait of his mentor.
Another friend and neighbor, Sam Polestro, kindly let us use his house
during the early preparations for the book. We thank them both.

For his help in defining the relationship between photographer and
press agent, I must thank my friend Harvey Sabinson, who incidentally
hired Eileen during his long and productive career.

Other people came to our aid in finding and identifying many of the
images; the first among them is Camille Dee, but also Rosalie Spar, Jeremy
Megraw, Jennifer Bright, and Drew Eliot. The staffs of the Museum of
the City of New York, the University of Washington, the Getty Museum,
and other institutions were also helpful. Unfortunately, not all of the
identifications were found, which meant that we had to rely on our mutual
deductions. We suspect that there are a few misidentifications, and we
apologize for those and hope that no offense is taken.

At Bulfinch Press, many thanks go to publisher Jill Cohen, associate
publisher Karen Murgolo, production manager Alyn Evans, and a special
thanks to our editor, Karyn Gerhard, for her guidance, support, and
unfailing belief in the project.

This book came into being because of the efforts of LTD, a group
of three remarkable women who are dedicated to publishing quality
editions on unusual but eminently worthy subjects. They are Jane Lahr,
Ann Tanenbaum, and Lyn DelliQuadri.

Finally, enormous gratitude and appreciation go to John Lynch.
His gifted art direction and perseverance in sifting through thousands
of photographs in Eileen Darby's archive ensures that her contribution
to theatrical history will be recognized and remembered.

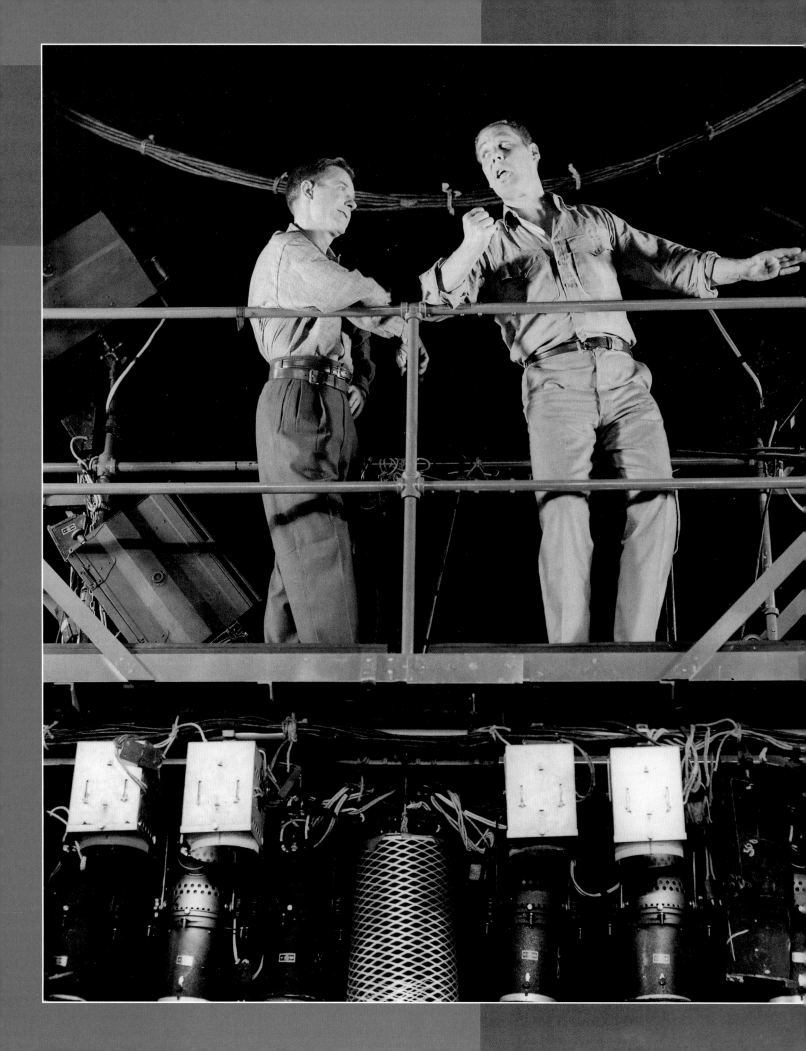

Contents

INTRODUCT

by John Lahr

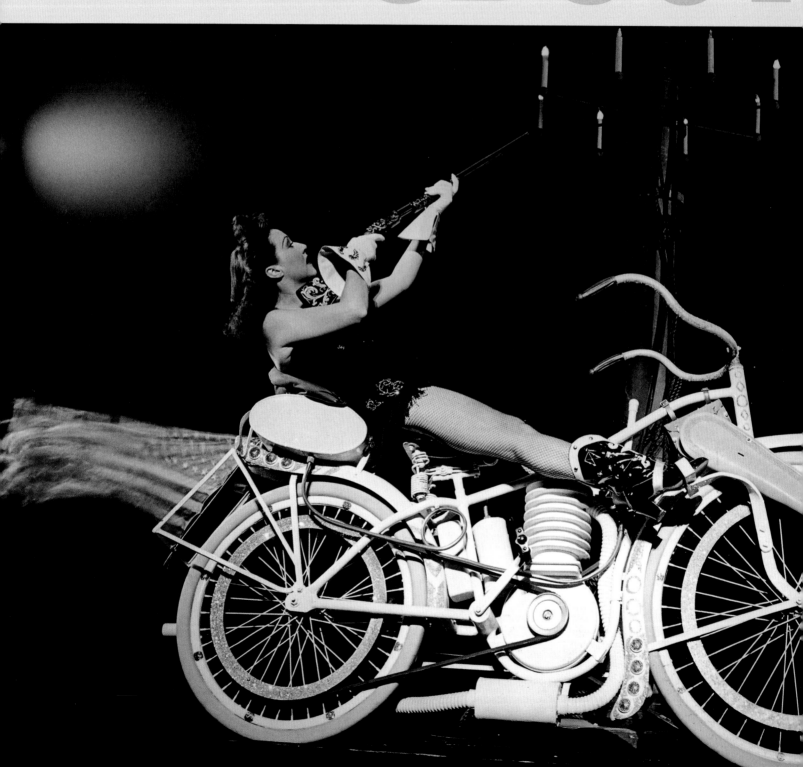

In Ambrose Bierce's sour definition, a photograph is "a picture painted by the sun without instruction in art." In her own crusty way, the eighty-seven-year-old theater photographer Eileen Darby would seem to agree. "It's not exactly a love affair," she said of the more than fifty years spent behind her Rolliflex. "You push the button on the camera. You hope you don't run out of film. And if your friends don't like it, they don't get a print."

Over the decades, on the covers of *Life* and in the nation's newspapers and magazines, Darby's photographs of the theater and theatricals have borne sensational witness to good times gone by. They are a sort of memory bank of the manners and moods of the time as well as of the great stars when the candle-power of their glow was high. Darby's first "candids"—photos taken from the first row of the theater during performance—were of Robert Sherwood's 1940 anti-Nazi melodrama, *There Shall Be No Night,* starring Alfred Lunt and Lynn Fontanne. "I almost didn't know who they were, but I still have that picture," Darby said. She continued: "If you get to see a show from the front row, how could you not like the job? If some guy sitting next to me got mad because I was annoying him with the click of a shutter, I didn't let it bother me. I wasn't thinking of style, I was thinking, 'I hope I got the right exposure.' " In her own way, like the people she photographed, Darby was in the business of show. "I needed pictures of the play, then somebody would buy them, then I would eat," she says. Although many of her photographs are iconic, Darby won't talk the folderol of art about her craft. "The thrill of taking photographs?" she says. "Being in the dark and developing the film and seeing that I got what I wanted. That's the thrill."

But what Darby wanted is where her artfulness resides. She had a strong sense of humor; her lens often found the energy of fun. Here, in bonnet and cigar, the morose Richard Rodgers is coaxed out of his gravity; with her raised shapely leg Agnes de Mille both answers and teases Elia Kazan's wired rigor; the comedienne Imogen Coca shows off the droll contradiction of

ABOVE: *Agnes de Mille and Elia Kazan rehearsing* One Touch of Venus *(1943).* *"Agnes is the most strong-minded theater artist I've ever known," Kazan wrote. "She was absolutely sure of what she wanted to do."*

LEFT: *Ethel Merman in* Annie Get Your Gun *(1946).* *"You break all the rules of nature," the actress Grace Moore told Merman about her singing. "Where does your breath come from?" "Necessity," Merman answered.*

her sweater-girl chest and her low comic puss; in preposterous Wagnerian regalia Bert Lahr caterwauls Comden and Green's show-stopping "Catch Our Act at the Met" from *Two on the Aisle,* the last of the great revues. Darby's intuitive grasp of graphic design and her instinct for the drama of line give compositional power to many of her photographs. Look at Ethel Merman in *Annie Get Your Gun.* Annie is putting out candles in her sharp-shooting circus act—Merman is turned into a streamlined piece of motorcycle machinery, her leg as straight and tapered as a piston. (We remember Merman as a fine sound; as we can see, she was also a fine shape.) The caprice of Bea Lillie, queen of the Broadway revue now forgotten in the hubbub of pop culture, is conjured merely by positioning Lillie's vertical hauteur to the side of the behemoth horizontal abstraction of her comic outline.

And then, of course, there's Marlon Brando as Stanley Kowalski in *Streetcar.* "I had a problem with Brando," Darby remembers. "A season or so before, I had photographed Paul Muni and there was this kid on stage who interrupted Muni's dialogue and who I thought was so rude. I told the kid, 'Go over to stage right and stand at the edge.' *Told* him! When I got into the darkroom, I cut the kid off. That was Brando. So when I shot *Streetcar* and saw that this kid was starring in it, I thought to myself, 'Now what am I gonna do?' But he behaved well this time." She continues: "I saw what was happening on stage, I knew what was to be taken, and I called for it." Here, in the sexual cat-and-mouse game between Stanley and Blanche, Darby's eye catches the immanence of both rape and seduction. Stanley may toy with his prey, but it's Blanche's hysterical acting out—the diamante tiara, the décolleté of her silk negligee, her panic-stricken desire—that brings out the sadist in him. Darby's photo has the gravity and sculpural definition of a frieze. Although the eye goes directly to Stanley, who stands in ambivalent equipoise above Blanche, it is she who controls the moment and the image, one of the most famous of modern theatrical photographs.

When Darby began taking photos with her Kodak Brownie in Portland, Oregon, she brought no point of view except enthusiasm to the enterprise. "If I saw something I took it," she says. "It's not that you wanted to be a photographer, it's that you wanted to record history." In the end, even unwittingly, her

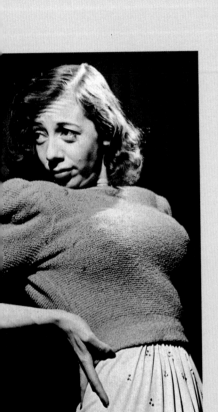

ABOVE: *Imogen Coca and her Lana Turner chest.*

RIGHT: *Bert Lahr and Dolores Gray singing "Catch Our Act at the Met," in* Two on the Aisle, *the last of the great revues (1952).*

photos achieve just that. Here, for instance, is Lillian Hellman before the carapace of pride and fame hardened her face into its fierce mask of vindictive triumph. Hellman is at ease in front of Darby's inquiring eye; she shows the camera the softer, less rebarbative, earnest side of her personality—the one that wrote more than eleven drafts of *The Little Foxes*. On the other hand, with his prickly intelligence on full display, Tennessee Williams stares down Darby's lens with a look that catches the steel underneath his vaunted softness. He is thin; he is chic; he is clear-eyed. He is in the flush of his new fame, only recently emerged from a decade of hard, penniless slog. How handsome and sure he looks at a rehearsal of *Streetcar,* whose script required almost no rewrites. Darby's portrait of Williams is choice because it records Williams renovated by his new fame but not yet claimed by it, before "the catastrophe of success," as he called it, bloated his body and lost his soul. In a time before endeavor turned to vainglory, sweetness is still evident in the youthful faces of many of the dynamic theatrical renegades Darby photographed—Elia Kazan, Jerome Robbins, and Leonard Bernstein among them.

Stars have to shine; like photographs, they use light and also create it. The poignancy of theater is its living moment. It has to be seen. It has to be experienced in the flesh. It is vividly in the moment; then, just as vividly, its brilliance vanishes. Photographs of theatricals both stop time and prove its glories. Here, for instance, you can feel the wattage of Merman's smile or the seduction of Mary Martin's apple-pie presence. Darby's camera is there to remember John Raitt at his beefcake best in *Carousel* and Laurette Taylor as Amanda Wingfield in *The Glass Menagerie,* a performance generally thought to be one of the greatest of the postwar period. "Her talent was luminous in a way that exceeded the natural," Tennessee Williams wrote of Taylor when she died in 1947. "Only once in a while and not long, the confusion and dimness about us thickly is penetrated by clarity, an illumination of this kind, which makes it possible to believe that the tunnel in which we live is not closed at both ends." Darby's theatrical photographs trap some of that original light and send it down the generations. They bear witness to both the short history and the joy of American stagecraft.

ABOVE: *Leonard Bernstein.*

RIGHT: *Laurette Taylor as Amanda in* The Glass Menagerie. *Tennessee Williams's four-character drama opened at the Playhouse Theatre on March 31, 1945.*

EILEEN DAR

A Life

In early May of 1940, a slim, young, and attractive photographer named Eileen Darby approached Victor Talley, the editor of the Rotogravure (picture) section of the Sunday edition of the *New York Times,* and asked him if he would be interested in seeing pictures of George M. Cohan (1878–1942), a Broadway celebrity who was trying out his new show in Pittsburgh. Talley replied that he would indeed be interested. Darby then called the press agent for the show, Charles Washburn, and asked for a front row seat so she could take candid photographs of the play as it unfolded. At her own expense, Darby traveled to the Nixon Theatre in Pittsburgh, where she shot *The Return of the Vagabond* in ambient light with her Leica. (Her camera lacked a light meter, which had only recently been invented, and for obvious reasons, Darby could not use a flash.) Back in New York, she quickly developed the pictures and took them to Talley, who bought exclusive rights to the group. She would discover later that buying pictures did not guarantee that they would be published.

On May 17, 1940, *The Return of the Vagabond* opened in New York in the National Theatre on West 41st Street but closed one day later after just three performances. A typical Cohan production, the play was written and produced by the great showman and featured him as the star performer. After the show closed, Cohan remarked to a friend, "They don't want me no more." It was his last appearance on the Broadway stage. Darby's only surviving image of Cohan shows him with a somewhat bemused expression on his face: one eye half-shut and lips compressed into a thin half-smile.

The Cohan photographs did not launch Darby's career as a theatrical photographer, but they did give her newfound confidence in her work. She would have to compete in a field crowded with both good and run-of-the-mill photographers, some of whom were formidable. At the top of the list was her former boss Alfred Eisenstaedt (1898–1995), who had worked for *Life* magazine since its inception. Other *Life* regulars such as Gjon Mili (1904–1984), John Swope (1908–1979), and Arnold Newman (b. 1918) already had established reputations.

ABOVE: *Eileen Darby entered the field of theatrical photography at the moment when George M. Cohan was exiting the theater. Although it was never published, this picture may be the only one that has survived of Cohan in* Return of the Vagabond.

LEFT: *The exuberant Carol Channing as Dolly Levi in* Hello, Dolly! *(1964) fairly bursts from this picture taken by Eileen Darby. It was the publicist's dream shot and was published far and wide.*

Darby's principal competition, however, was the Vandamm studio, which was favored by producers and press agents alike. A transplanted Londoner, Florence Vandamm (1883–1966) managed the studio with her American husband, George Robert Thomas (1887–1944), who was known in the photographic corps as Tommy Vandamm. In their heyday, the Vandamms photographed the vast majority of productions that made it to Broadway, and they ferociously guarded their turf. When Tommy Vandamm died in 1944, he left a vacuum that many photographers moved quickly to fill.

Armed with her Leica and the chutzpah she acquired in New York City, Darby seized the opportunity created by Tommy Vandamm's absence. By obtaining tickets to shows and shooting them (under the nose of the aging Florence, who had taken her late husband's place), she gradually began to receive assignments from theatrical press agents. One of these agents, Bernard Simon, remembered her clambering over rows of seats with shoulder bags flying as she fired away shots of the action on stage. Simon credited Darby with taking the first candid pictures that were coming into favor and replacing the posed, retouched pictures produced by the Vandamms.

The theatrical press agent was, and remains, the meal ticket for theatrical photographers, since the agent is responsible for selecting the photographer for each show. If the show is a hit, both the press agent and the photographer benefit financially from its success. One of the legendary press agents of the 1940s and 1950s was Richard Maney, who, in his autobiography, *Fanfare,* describes the ideal photographer:

> [The press agent] seeks an experienced photographer rather than an inspired one. The nominee should be tactful and conditioned to the moods and megrims of his opponents. He must know how to cajole them into compliance. To approximate the sixty or seventy negatives needed, press agent and cameraman must have the cooperation of players, stagehands, and above all the stage manager . . . whose job was to have the players available when called.

Maney goes on to say that the press agent and the photographer work together to plot the pictures, which entails selecting a few lines of dialogue for the actors to exchange as pictures are snapped. He notes that all of the pictures must be

ABOVE: *Dick Maney was the publicist for all but one of Tallulah Bankhead's shows. He once wrote: "Offstage and on, she has a style and tang and bravura that set her apart." Her contract for Philip Barry's* Foolish Notion *stipulated Maney as her publicist. According to him, Bankhead turned many bad plays into hits because her legion of fans bought tickets to anything she starred in.*

RIGHT: *Eileen Darby's photograph made her look glamorous and svelte.*

taken in the time allotted by the theatrical unions, usually four hours for a play and five hours for a musical. At that time, photographs were shot in the tryout city, which was usually—but not always—New Haven, Connecticut. Shooting commenced the minute the audience left the theater following a performance. When the actors returned to the stage, Darby would begin taking pictures with a hand-held camera and move to a larger camera on a tripod if a picture of the entire stage was required. These pictures were added to the images Darby had already taken during the performance from her seat in the first row.

Occasionally, a press agent would have a favorite photographer. For instance, Richard Maney called on George Karger at least a dozen times because he liked the way Karger worked. Judging by the number of shows Darby shot for him, Maney must have enjoyed working with her as well. Over the years, he gave her some plum photographic assignments; some of the shows were flops, but others were big hits, including *Foolish Notion* (a Tallulah Bankhead tour de force), *Gentlemen Prefer Blondes* (a Carol Channing vehicle), *Gigi* (the show that introduced Audrey Hepburn to Broadway), and *Watch on the Rhine* (Lillian Hellman's anti-Nazi play).

In Darby's day, press agents selected photographers for a variety of reasons, the most important being their ability to take pictures with speed and efficiency. The photographers' artistic merits were rarely considered. In the crowded field of photographers operating then, the personality of the picture taker was almost as important as his or her skills in photography. This led Eisenstaedt to remark that "it's more important to click with people than to click the shutter." Darby was unusual in her ability to click a shutter and click with theater people well. She claimed to have fallen into theatrical photography because she had "more luck than brains." She also insisted, with a straight face, that picture-taking was a good way to obtain free tickets to shows.

Darby's fascination with photography and the camera began as a child in Portland, Oregon. The daughter of John and Lillian Darby, Eileen learned the art of photography literally at her father's knee. John Darby was more than an amateur photographer. A civil engineer by profession, he worked for the federal government as a draftsman and routinely took pictures of projects for which he was preparing drawings. He believed that pictures constituted an important

record of an event, whether the event was the construction of a dam or the gathering of a family. He owned two large Kodak cameras, one of which took 4 x 5" negatives and the other, 6 x 8" negative plates. The latter was made of wood and didn't have a shutter. When John Darby photographed his family with this camera, he would order them to stop breathing while he lifted the cap from the lens, exposed the plate for a few seconds, and recapped the lens long enough to extract the plate from the camera. He both developed the negatives and made the final prints, skills that he taught his daughter. Darby has retained her father's cameras out of nostalgia.

Darby was no ordinary girl. While other girls her age were playing with dolls, she busied herself snapping pictures. Like many Americans, Darby owned a Kodak Box Brownie, but unlike them, she was developing the photographs shot with this camera herself. By age twelve, she was so adept at developing negatives and printing images that her mother allowed her to build a darkroom in the basement from wood she salvaged from the Columbia River. To earn money to buy film and materials, the ever-enterprising Darby would venture down to Portland's docks to meet the passenger ships and to sell their patrons *Liberty* magazine, an extremely popular news magazine of the era.

In time, Darby became acquainted with other camera enthusiasts. One of them, Herb Alden, operated a small commercial studio in Portland. Whenever a fire broke out or an accident occurred, Alden and his camera were not far away. If a visit to the studio coincided with one of these events, Darby would hop on the back of Alden's motorcycle and ride off with him to witness the action. She would carefully observe how he shot the pictures that he hoped to sell to the local press. Eventually, Alden was successful in selling his pictures and was hired by the *Portland Journal*.

In 1935, Darby went to work in the camera department of the local emporium Lipman Wolfe, where she had the opportunity to meet other professional photographers, including Ernst Kassowitz (1888–1983). A native of Vienna, Kassowitz had a European accent that delighted Darby. But she was even more impressed by the several 35 mm Leica cameras in his possession. In 1930, just five years after the invention of the 35 mm camera, Kassowitz had begun taking photographs professionally with his Leicas, then the rage of the camera world. In 1935, Kassowitz immigrated to the

ABOVE: *Eileen as a babe in arms (right), held by her mother, Lillian Borquist Darby, with her sister, Patricia. The family was very tightly knit, and Eileen continued to make trips across country to see them as often as she could.*

United States, settling first in New York and then embarking on a peripatetic existence that included Chicago, Milwaukee, and eventually Portland and Port Angeles, Washington. When Darby met Kassowitz, he had just relocated to Portland from Milwaukee.

Charmed by Darby's good looks and energy, Kassowitz took her under his wing. He invited Darby to his studio, where she learned about photographic chemicals and paper and the virtue of patience in photography. If he had questionable motives in mentoring her, Darby was impervious to them.

By that time, Darby had graduated to a Kodak folding camera, an improvement over her old Brownie. She was ecstatic when Kassowitz invited her to go with him to photograph a ballet company at the Paramount Theatre in Portland. He loaned her one of his Leicas and both of them shot pictures during the performance. To her surprise and delight, her pictures were superior to those taken by Kassowitz. Darby was disappointed, however, when she was unable to sell any to the local press. She believed that selling a picture would signal her arrival as a professional photographer.

Darby finally got her lucky break. One night, as she was driving across a bridge in Portland, she saw flames and smoke in the distance. She quickly pulled over, climbed up a telephone pole, straddled the cross arm of the pole, and took long shots of the fire. After developing the images, Darby brought the best one to the editor of the *Portland Telegram*, who bought it on the spot, paying her three dollars. This event was an important milestone in her life.

Darby never doubted that she would become a professional photographer, but she received no real training except for what she gleaned from her father, Ernst Kassowitz, and other local professionals. For her general education, her devoutly religious parents sent Darby to Portland's Catholic schools. To nourish their daughter's athletic side, the Darbys enrolled her in swimming classes. As a child, Darby learned how to swim in Portland's public pools and then trained at the Multnomah Athletic Club, where she excelled under the tutelage of the swimming coach there. Her energy and natural athleticism led her to win numerous statewide meets and eventually helped her gain admittance to Marylhurst College, located in a Portland suburb. By chance the college needed a

ABOVE: *Although John Darby was an amateur photographer, he had the zeal and the discipline of a professional. Even when he was taking pictures of his family with his cumbersome wood camera, he made sure that all of the elements were correct.*

BELOW LEFT: *Eileen enjoyed sports and competitions. During her years in high school and college, she excelled in swimming and won many statewide meets. This picture was taken while Eileen was competing in the Junior National Swimming Meet in San Francisco.*

BELOW RIGHT: *She also fenced at Marylhurst College, although it is not known whether she took home any medals in the sport. This picture was taken by Herb Alden, a professional Portland photographer who befriended Eileen.*

swimming instructor and offered her admittance and free tuition in exchange for giving lessons to students. More than once in her life, Darby relied on her champion swimming to keep her financially afloat.

Although she enjoyed her college days, Darby never completed a degree at Marylhurst. Instead, a friend named Pat Cavanaugh stepped in to alter her fate. An art student at Marylhurst, Cavanaugh hankered to go to New York and eventually found a way to realize her dream. She applied for, and won, a scholarship to a New York art school and then prevailed upon Darby to accompany her. Realizing a move to New York might further her career as a photographer, Darby agreed and announced her plans to her mother. Mrs. Darby's only comment was: "Eileen, you better go downtown and buy a winter coat because it's cold there."

Darby bought the winter coat and was soon waving good-bye to her family from a train bound east. The two young women arrived in New York in 1937 during the dying throes of the Great Depression. After they found an inexpensive walk-up flat, Cavanaugh attended art school while Darby searched for a job. Armed with a recommendation letter from Kassowitz to a friend of his at Leitz, the company that made Leica cameras, she presented herself at their New York offices. That contact sent her to Pix, a photographic agency founded by Eisenstaedt and Werner Wolfe, who were considered two of the finest photojournalists in the country. They offered Darby a position in the darkroom.

Darby's job was to assist in processing the film of the photographers on staff at Pix. Her Irish charm got her through the door, but her knowledge of professional processing fell somewhat short. Luckily, a young photographer named Cornell Capa (b. 1918) was willing to teach her the ropes. Darby would rely on the skills she learned from Capa throughout her life. Eventually, thanks to Capa's instruction and her own hard work, Darby's darkroom skills became legendary.

As a result of their shared experiences at Pix, Darby and Capa became lifelong friends. Many years later, in 1974, Capa, out of a desire to bring respectability to the art of photography, founded the International Center of Photography in New York. His older brother, Robert Capa (1913–1954), another Pix employee, was the famed World War II photographer who lost his life on the Indochina front in 1954. When he died, Robert Capa left an almost unparalleled photographic record of the war.

Most of the people on staff at Pix, including Eisenstaedt,

ABOVE: *At Pix, she learned the finer points of processing photographs from her darkroom coworkers Cornell Capa (left) and Werner Wolf (right). It is possible that this photograph was taken by their boss, the great Alfred Eisenstaedt, in November 1937.*

TOP: *It was in 1940 that Eileen's career as a theatrical photographer began in earnest. She had the good fortune to start with interesting (if not successful) plays to shoot. In Portland, she caught Paul Robeson in* John Henry *on tour.*

CENTER: *In the early 1940s, Gregory Peck was still unknown and Eileen Darby had the good fortune to catch him at this time in summer stock. In 1942, Peck made his Broadway debut in a short-lived play called* The Morning Star, *which Darby photographed. Pictured are Peck and Gladys Cooper being directed by Guthrie McClintock.*

BOTTOM: *Montgomery Clift was a child actor on Broadway and eventually graduated to adult roles. One of the earliest was in Robert Sherwood's* There Shall Be No Night, *which Eileen Darby photographed. The love interest in the play is provided by Clift as Erik and Elisabeth Fraser as Kaatri.*

were Jewish refugees from Europe who had fled Hitler's wrath. Although she greatly admired this influential photographer and his work, Darby had little contact with Eisenstaedt, except on the occasions when he would stop in the darkroom to admonish her: "You must dust, Miss Darby, always dust." If a speck of dust landed in the enlarger, a large blob would mar the resulting print.

Several of Darby's coworkers, dissatisfied with their lot at Pix, wanted to break away and start their own agency. She was warned by Eisenstaedt not to join forces with the rebels, but exercising her fierce independence, she threw in her lot with her coworkers and left Pix. Unfortunately, their new agency almost immediately shut down when, after three short weeks, the photographers failed to pay the rent. Darby found herself out of a job. She worked briefly as a salesgirl in a department store and then went back to Portland for the summer to work as a lifeguard.

Darby returned to New York wiser and somewhat chastened. She realized that she would have to make her own way in the competitive world of photojournalism. By this time, she had acquired a used Leica that allowed her to shoot better, more professional pictures. Of course, snapping good pictures proved easier than selling them to magazines and newspapers. Occasionally she got lucky, but most of the time, she did not. As a result, in 1939 she and Joel Lapidus, another former coworker at Pix, decided to set up an agency on East 28th Street in Manhattan, which eventually became Graphic House. Lapidus assumed the responsibility of shooting the pictures and Darby processed the film.

By the early 1940s, Darby was eager to find more work in the theater. She received an assignment to shoot the antiwar drama *There Shall Be No Night* (1940) from Bill Fields, one of the best press agents on Broadway. The play, written by the Pulitzer Prize winner Robert Sherwood and produced by two very active and influential Broadway groups, the Theatre Guild and the Playwrights Company, starred Alfred Lunt and Lynn Fontanne and featured Richard Whorf, Sidney Greenstreet, and a very young Montgomery Clift. This big break, coupled with her happy memories of photographing the ballet in Portland and Paul Robeson during his tour of *John Henry* in 1936, made Darby realize that she had an affinity for theatrical photography and should make it her specialty. All that she needed were calls from press agents.

The 1940s could not have been a more propitious time for Darby to embark on her new career. Broadway was on the verge of entering a great and special period in its history. The decades immediately following World War II, in particular, encompassed what many consider to be the golden age of the American theater. The foundations for this golden age were laid in the period from 1920 to 1940, years when American playwrights began attracting the world's attention. This era was dominated by Eugene O'Neill (1883–1953), who won the Nobel Prize in 1936, and it also included Maxwell Anderson (1888–1959), Lillian Hellman (1905–1984), George S. Kaufman (1889–1961), Clifford Odets (1906–1963), Elmer Rice (1892–1967), and Thornton Wilder (1897–1975), all of whom made remarkable contributions to the stage. These luminaries paved the way for the next generation of American playwrights, which included Edward Albee (b. 1928), Robert Anderson (b. 1917), William Inge (1913–1973), Arthur Miller (b. 1915), and Tennessee Williams (1911–1983).

American musical theater showed similar signs of vitality and innovation. Following the appearance of Jerome Kern and Oscar Hammerstein's *Show Boat* in 1927 and George Gershwin's *Porgy and Bess* in 1935, musical theater abandoned European operetta models, which seemed artificial, and evolved into a uniquely American art form. They created realistic American themes, used indigenous musical modes, and integrated the songs with the story. The contributions made by Richard Rodgers (1902–1979) with both Lorenz Hart (1895–1960) and Oscar Hammerstein II (1895–1960), and by Irving Berlin (1888–1989), Jerome Kern (1885–1945), Alan Jay Lerner (1918–1986) with Frederick Loewe (1901–1988), Frank Loesser (1910–1969), Cole Porter (1891–1964), Stephen Sondheim (b. 1930), Jule Styne (1905–1994), and others too numerous to mention ushered in an unprecedented era of magnificent musical theater. The coming of age of the American theater on all fronts had begun, and Darby brilliantly captured its history and magical moments with her arresting photographs.

In the 1940s, Darby began receiving more and more calls from press agents such as Richard Maney and William Fields, Samuel Friedman, Sol Jacobson, Ben Kornzweig, and James D. Proctor. These men all belonged to a generation of outstanding press agents who were handling most of the great

ABOVE: *On one of the occasions when she was out in the field, she scored a coup when she took a series of shots of Mayor Fiorello LaGuardia and his son at a big league baseball game—unbeknownst to them—and sold them to* Life, *the premier picture magazine (founded by Henry Luce in 1936) that had been built on great photojournalism. Eileen Darby recorded their emotions at the game so skillfully that she won the 1942 U.S. Camera Award for the series.*

shows. At this time, Graphic House, the agency Darby helped found, also was growing as other photographers joined its ranks.

During the early 1940s, several events occurred that would permanently change Darby's life and career. While at a ball game at Yankee Stadium one afternoon, she noticed Mayor LaGuardia sitting with his son in one of the boxes. She surreptitiously shot numerous pictures of the colorful mayor, which caught the changing expressions on his face as he reacted to the action on the ball field and to his son. Darby immediately developed the photographs and presented them as a series to the picture editors at *Life,* hoping they would find one or two worthy of publication. The editors bought the entire series, which appeared in the July 21, 1941, issue. Later, the pictures were reprinted in *U.S. Camera* and won that magazine's award for the year's best photographs. Thereafter, whenever Mayor LaGuardia saw Darby with her camera, he never failed to greet her.

Publication in *Life* was the goal of every photographer and the mark of his or her arrival in the field of photojournalism. The brainchild of Henry Luce, *Life* was founded in 1936 as a weekly picture magazine. Eisenstaedt, Margaret Bourke-White (1904–1971), Thomas D. McAvoy (1905–1966), and Peter Stackpole (1913–1997) were the first staff photographers. After his stint at Graphic House, Joel Lapidus, now known as Yale Joel, joined the staff, as did Darby's old friend Cornell Capa. Shortly after the LaGuardia pictures were published, Darby began receiving assignments from *Life* and was even offered a staff position at the magazine, but she turned down the offer cold when she discovered that the women photographers on staff made half the salary of the male photographers. She did, however, gratefully accept the assignments. For *Life*'s entertainment pages, she shot José Ferrer making himself up as Cyrano de Bergerac and such important Broadway premieres in the 1940s and 1950s as *Annie Get Your Gun, Carousel, Death of a Salesman, Guys and Dolls,* and *A Streetcar Named Desire.* Darby's favorite *Life* assignment and one of her treasured experiences was going to London in 1945 to shoot Old Vic productions before they went to Broadway. Not only did she photograph the plays and the rehearsals, she shot portraits of the stars and stars in the making.

Gradually, Graphic House became known for the quality

One of the most memorable and enjoyable assignments of Eileen Darby's career as a photographer was going to London for Life to shoot the Old Vic Theatre Company in 1946, before their arrival in New York. She was at liberty to shoot whatever and whomever she wanted, both on and off stage—and did.

LEFT: *In their dressing rooms (left to right), Laurence Olivier making up as Mr. Puff and Ralph Richardson as Lord Burleigh, in Richard Brinsley Sheridan's* The Critic.

of its film processing, and photographers began to leave their film at the agency. As a result, Darby became acquainted with many local photographers, including Nina Leen, whom she greatly admired. On one occasion, Leen brought her brother Roy Lester, newly arrived from Germany, to the agency. The surnames Lester and Leen were derived from the family name of Lessnik, which each sibling chose to adapt. Originally from Odessa, the family relocated to Germany in the aftermath of the Russian Revolution (1917) when it became clear that the new government was antagonistic toward organized religions. Devoutly Russian Orthodox, the Lessnik family felt compelled to emigrate. Darby looked at Roy in his long camel hair coat and thought that he could pass for actor Peter Lorre's younger brother.

Roy Lester was also a professional photographer and, despite Darby's first impression of him, a handsome man. After immersing himself in the study of English, he joined the staff at Graphic House and began selling Darby and Joel's pictures. By degrees, he took over the functions of a manager and eventually was running the agency. In 1943, Lester moved it to 149 East 40th Street, on the ground floor of an apartment house. Five years later, he set up the agency in more professional quarters at 280 Madison Avenue.

In 1944, Darby and Lester decided that their business partnership was working so well that they should make it more permanent. Whether Lester married *his* boss or Darby married *hers* is known only to the principals involved. Theirs was a long, happy, and fruitful marriage that produced four children, Virginia, Roy Jr., John Gregori, and Patric. Realizing his wife's assignments would take her far from family, Lester welcomed into their home a trio of sisters from Germany, who took over childcare and domestic duties. In addition to traveling for work, Darby returned to Portland every few years, sometimes with her children in tow, to visit family and friends.

In 1942, Darby formed another important lifelong connection. Through various family contacts, a high school student named Murray Garrett obtained an appointment with Lester to discuss a possible job. At the time, Garrett was packing ladies' hats, but his heart was in photography. Lester offered Garrett a job for less money, but he took it anyway, in order to learn an art and skill at a prestigious agency. At first, Garrett's duties involved running and fetching, but eventually he moved into the darkroom, where his serious study of film processing began under Darby's tutelage. When she deemed him ready, Darby also instructed Garrett in taking good pictures. Eventually, she took him along as her assistant on her assignments. Garrett marveled at Darby's photographic skills but was most impressed by the way she handled people. If ever there was a time when Darby's heritage served her well, it was during the photo calls. She was an amalgam of her Irish father, who had wit and charm to spare, and her indomitable Swedish mother. She needed all these qualities in her dealings with theater people. To this day, Garrett remembers with admiration both Darby's formidable people and photographic skills within the limited time frame of the photo call—a good theatrical photographer had to shoot fast and furiously.

Darby's particular talent lay in her ability to capture the myriad emotions being expressed on stage, as well as the essence of a particular scene, which gave life to her pictures. By showing actors speaking, singing, and dancing, she managed to actualize the theatrical experience and to avoid the posed look of traditional stage photography. Harvey Sabinson, the heir to the previous generation of legendary press agents, writes the following about Darby's unique contribution to theatrical photography:

> Eileen Darby, probably more than any other photographer, was responsible for the transition from the frozen, retouched still lifes of the twenties and thirties to representations of real living performers doing their thing onstage. When she shot *Hello, Dolly!* for me, she had the responsibility of making a larger-than-life star, Carol Channing, appear just that way. And she succeeded admirably, while producing a collection of photographs that made my work as the show's publicist easier. Who can forget the famous photo of Carol about to start down the staircase of the Harmonia Gardens for the *Hello, Dolly!* title song?
> That photo fairly sings out. Now that's art.

Whenever possible, Darby tried to capture the personality of the character the actor was portraying. In one of her most powerful images of *A Streetcar Named Desire,* the brutish quality of Marlon Brando's Stanley is revealed. Brando's body curves menacingly over a kneeling and terrorized Blanche (Jessica Tandy), whose fright is visible in her eyes. The

OVERLEAF: *During the London assignment, Darby had time to do a little sightseeing and had her picture taken with a sphinx.*

BELOW: *Eileen Darby and her husband backstage at the production of* Inside U.S.A. *in 1948.*

beauty of these candid photographs lies in the way they show the intensity and drama of a particular moment on stage and manage to transform the actors into real people.

During a photo call, Darby would position the floodlights to brighten as much of the stage as possible. To augment her lighting, she would ask stagehands to train spotlights on particular areas of the stage. Though she disliked flashbulbs, Darby used them when necessary, particularly in shooting close-ups. Darby was greatly relieved when the more dependable electronic strobe light came into use since it would flash automatically at the exact moment the shutter was released.

Darby knew that both stage luminaries and stagehands were not the world's most well-behaved citizens. She was prepared for the displays of temper and dissatisfaction that occasionally erupted. Undaunted, Darby responded with tact, civility, and a twinkle in her eye, letting everyone know she was a professional and an equal—*and in charge*. Refusing to be intimidated, she tackled the job at hand and received the cooperation and respect of star and stagehand alike.

Dressed in pants and a shirt, Darby exuded confidence and efficiency when she walked on stage to give instructions and explain the photo session. The performers listened to her, and she listened intently to their comments and suggestions. The session shots were planned in an earlier meeting with the press agent, but Darby knew unforeseen possibilities for good pictures might emerge later. Darby shot most of her pictures with a Rolliflex, the professional camera of choice, but when she needed to shoot actors against a backdrop, she used a Speed-Graphic camera on a tripod. With this camera, Darby was able to take in as much of the set as possible. One of the pictures she shot with her Speed-Graphic is among her most widely reproduced and has achieved iconic status. The image, which shows the skeletonized Loman house in *Death of a Salesman*, instantly conveys the idea that the play is about peering into the life of a family as if it were taking an X-ray of its members' souls.

After the photo call, Darby and Garrett would dash from the theater in the tryout town, whether New Haven, Boston, or Washington, to catch the next train to New York. Back at the agency, Garrett would stay up all night if necessary to develop the film and produce the prints so that Darby could bring them to the press agent the following morning. The agent would pick out his or her favorite shots, have reprints made, and distribute them in a press kit to the drama page reporters. Some of the pictures landed on *Playbill* covers and souvenir books, others on posters and heralds (one-page sheets stacked in public places). The agent was especially pleased when a picture appeared in a newspaper or magazine, since that meant free publicity for the show.

Before there were radio commercials, television spots, film clips, or video, there was the photograph, the tangible record of a performance of a play or musical. From the beginning of the history of photography, the theater world embraced the new medium with complete enthusiasm. Louis-Jacques-Mandé Daguerre, a scene designer by profession, invented a process that captured an image on a silver-coated copper plate. He called this proto-photograph a daguerreotype. His experiments and the work of his successors unleashed an unending series of related inventions.

The art of the daguerreotype quickly crossed the ocean to the United States, where many took it up. When P. T. Barnum (1810–1891), perhaps the greatest promoter of all time, ushered Jenny Lind (1820–1887) into the studio of the pioneer photographer Mathew Brady (1823–1896) to be daguerreotyped, the theater and photography worlds fortuitously collided. Barnum had the resulting daguerreotype lithographed so that multiple copies of the image could be made and distributed. Barnum widely disseminated Brady's likeness of Lind, inspiring the world to flock to the theater to hear her sing and filling his own coffers.

Numerous technical advances brought the photograph into everyone's life, but most tellingly into the lives of stage actors. Well aware of the publicity value of their likenesses, both workaday actors and stars of the stage patronized professional photographers. Before the invention of photography, only the faces and figures of the most prominent actors were immortalized in paintings and drawings. Hence, almost no images exist documenting the work and lives of the lesser-known actor.

In the mid-nineteenth century, professional photographers were confined to their studios, where they would use the light streaming down through skylights to take photographs. But the moment was not far off when these photographers could work in the theater. In 1883, a photographer personally supervised by Thomas Edison used electric lights strung across the stage to take the first photographs of an indoor stage. But several years elapsed before electric lighting was installed in theaters, thus allowing photographers to document the action on stage.

One other element was needed to complete the evolution in stage photography—the means to create a sudden "flash" or burst of light to produce detailed images of the actors and the sets. Englishman Joseph Byron (1846–1922) was one of the first photographers to use flash photography. Byron arrived in New York in 1883, set up his studio, and within a few years was capturing on glass plates most of the productions appearing on Broadway. In the theater, Byron would set up an 11 x 14" camera on a platform in front of the stage and scatter his assistants around the auditorium. When he wanted to take pictures, Byron would command his assistants to ignite the inflammable powder, which set off flashes of light. Eventually, Byron began the tradition of taking pictures in the tryout towns so that they would be ready to publish on opening night in New York.

Byron left a peerless record of the New York stage from 1881 to 1910, the period when he was routinely photographing all aspects of the theater. After his death, the studio founded by Luther White, which had been a rival for some years, took over Byron's business. The studio improved flash photography and began the practice of printing "key sheets"—pages of reduced prints similar to today's contact sheets from which producers or stars could make a selection.

According to historian Naomi Rosenblum, about twenty-five hundred women photographers were receiving jobs and assignments around 1915, and not merely winning recognition and prizes. Their presence both behind the camera and in the darkroom was necessary at this time. Once the photograph could be reproduced in print, the demand for images to accompany stories in newspapers, magazines, and books became almost impossible to satisfy. The rise of advertising in the 1920s also increased the country's insatiable appetite for illustrations of all kinds, particularly photographs, since they were used to hawk products. As a result of these changes, women photographers came into their own during this period.

The photographer Florence Vandamm (1883–1966), mentioned earlier as a formidable rival to Darby and the other "new blood" coming into the field, abandoned her career as a portrait painter in London in order to learn photography. Shortly thereafter, she set up a studio. In 1918, Florence Vandamm married George Robert Thomas (1887–1944), to whom she taught all that she knew about photography. In 1923, they decided to pull up stakes and move to New York. Assignments in the United States from *Vogue* and *Vanity Fair* to photograph theater celebrities led to more theater work and a specialization in the field.

Within a few years, the Vandamms were shooting about seventy-five percent of all the productions that appeared on Broadway. Following Tommy's death in 1944, Florence and her assistants continued the business, working both in the studio and in the theater. Then, in 1955, Florence retreated into her studio for the rest of her active career. In 1961, she closed her business and retired, selling her negatives and prints to the New York Public Library of the Performing Arts, where they are an important component of the Billy Rose Theatre Collection.

Although the work of her studio marked a milestone in theatrical photography, Florence was not the first woman to photograph the stars. That honor belongs to the wife of Aimé Dupont, whose specialty was photographing stars of the Metropolitan Opera and occasionally of the Broadway stage. Following her husband's death, she took over his studio and continued his work. These two dynamic women, Dupont and Vandamm, paved the way for other women.

Darby continued the tradition of women in theatrical photography. Although her work accounted for half of Graphic House's business, the agency also received commissions for all types of general and journalistic photography. In 1946, Darby and Lester decided to open a branch of their business in California and hired Murray Garrett to run the new office. It turned out to be a highly successful venture as Garrett began to receive assignments from major West Coast publications. Eventually, with Darby and Lester's blessings, Garrett and a partner set up their own business, with Graphic House acting as their agent. In recent years, two handsome books of Garrett's celebrity portraits have been published.

For a period of nearly thirty years, Darby's theatrical photographs appeared in newspapers in New York and throughout the country. Six of these photographs made the cover of *Life*. Others were featured in such notable publications as *Look,* the *New York Times Magazine, Newsweek, Redbook,*

ABOVE: *A candid shot of Eileen taken by Kate Cahill, a longtime friend and wife of her doctor, Kevin Cahill, at the annual art show in Point Lookout, New York, in the late 1990s. (Some of Darby's photographs were displayed in the show.) She made her home in Point Lookout for many years and was a familiar figure to most of the residents.*

the *Saturday Evening Post, Theatre Arts, Time,* and *U.S. Camera.* In the section of Tom Prideaux's *World Theatre in Pictures* devoted to modern theater, Darby is represented by no fewer than twenty-two pictures—more than any other photographer.

In the 1950s, a large number of people entered the field of stage photography just as the number of productions on Broadway began to shrink drastically. As a result, fewer and fewer opportunities were available for the photographic corps. The press agents who knew Darby continued to call on her, valuing her dependability and sharp eye, but a new generation of press agents was emerging as the old agents retired, and Darby was unknown to them.

Martha Swope emerged in the 1960s as the next prominent female photographer of the stage. Swope was a dancer who turned her hobby of photographing her fellow ballet dancers into a full-time career of dance and theatrical photography. When Swope retired, two young women succeeded her. One of them, Joan Marcus, began her career in the darkroom at the Kennedy Center in Washington, processing the film of the center's official photographer. Eventually Marcus became the official photographer. Later, to broaden her sphere of activities, she moved to New York, where she continues to live and work. Carol Rosegg, Swope's former assistant, travels throughout the country on assignments to photograph productions.

Graphic House began to fade when Lester died in 1976, and Darby grew less interested in Broadway. She dates her disaffection with Broadway to the appearance in 1968 of *Hair,* the popular rock musical about a group of hippies. However, Darby did not immediately pack up her cameras and quietly steal away. Taking pictures remained a vital part of her life. She continued to make prints in her darkroom to send to writers and publishers and to carry a camera with her everywhere in case a face or sight caught her fancy. Whenever she met a friend or neighbor as she walked along the streets of Point Lookou , New York, her home for the past forty years, she would pull a wad of pictures from her pocket and hand over a photograph of the person, of his or her home or favorite pet, taken on a previous day.

Darby's priceless collection of negatives and prints are stored in what she referred to as the "file room," which is filled with boxes containing unknown treasures and file cabinets stuffed with folders devoted to the shows she photographed. Her pictures can also be found in the files of the Billy Rose Theatre Collection of the New York Public Library of the Performing Arts, where students, scholars, writers, and journalists can pore over her work and continue to marvel over its raw power.

The curator of this collection, Robert Taylor, eloquently summarizes Darby's unique contribution to theatrical photography:

> The Billy Rose Theatre Collection houses nearly three million photographs of theater artists and theatrical productions. Dozens of outstanding photographers are represented in this collection, among them the Vandamms, Friedman Abeles, Martha Swope, to name only three. Each photographer has uniqueness, a trademark look, and in the photographs of Eileen Darby, the look is one of animation, vitality, and of the moment. Eileen was active during one of the richest periods of American theatre, and at the time, she was one of the few—or perhaps the only—major photographers employing this caught-in-action technique, which has become the norm for theatrical photographers. To have twenty-five years of American theater documented in photographs of such truth and immediacy is a gift to history for which theater historians and publishers are today overwhelmingly grateful. Eileen's photographs are in great demand by the Library's researchers and are among the most requested for broadcast and publication. Her photographic legacy will be treasured for generations to come.

THE *Shows*

LEFT: The cast of *Bloomer Girl* (1944), shot from a
box in the theater during a performance.
ABOVE: Celeste Holm (*center*) and Joan McCracken
(*foreground*) from the ballet school scene in
Bloomer Girl (1944).

Anne of England

THE PLOT OF *Anne of England* tells of a tangle of intrigue at the court of Queen Anne (1665–1714). Although beautifully acted, critics were not kind to the Mary Cass Canfield and Ethel Borden play. As a result, the public stayed away and it closed a week after opening on October 7, 1941. It did, however, give Eileen Darby the opportunity to photograph Flora Robson, who played the Duchess of Marlborough, the character at the center of the intrigue. Jessica Tandy was cast as her cousin, Abigail Hill. Tandy commuted from London to appear in this play and many others before finally settling in New York.

LEFT: A young caricaturist named Al Hirschfeld sketches Jessica Tandy on the set of the play.

RIGHT: The very regal Flora Robson, looking every inch a duchess.

The Pirate

IT IS DOUBTFUL that audiences flocked to *The Pirate* because of its plot, which to say the least was convoluted and sometimes downright silly in spite of being the work of playwright S. N. Behrman. The attraction of course was the Lunts—Alfred Lunt and Lynn Fontanne, whose expert acting and interaction alone were worth the price of admission. The Playwrights Company teamed with the Theatre Guild to produce the comedy, which was staged by Lunt himself in 1952.

ABOVE: Lunt with Lea Penman and Lynn Fontanne.

Wine, Women and Song

WINE, WOMEN AND SONG was described as a "revue-vaudeville-burlesque show" and it was indeed probably all three. Margie Hart was a graduate of the burlesque stage, while Jimmy Savo, Pinkie Lee, Herbie Faye, and others in the cast spent time in vaudeville, burlesque, and revues. Lee Shubert, I. H. Herk, and Max Liebman produced this concoction, which was supervised by Liebman and directed by Murray Friedman. Even with all of the great talent on stage, the production, which opened on September 28, 1942, ran only 150 performances.

LEFT: Margie Hart and Jimmy Savo in a bit of burlesque buffoonery.

Oklahoma!

IS THERE ANYONE in the world today who does not know *Oklahoma!?* This now-legendary musical not only changed the course of the American musical but also represented the first teaming of Richard Rodgers and Oscar Hammerstein and led to a string of works that remain unsurpassed in theatrical history. It also brought to the stage the spirited and brilliant Agnes de Mille, whose dances thrilled audiences for their originality and balletic qualities. The opening night, March 9, 1943, was a triumph for everyone involved, from the Theatre Guild, which produced it, to the director, Rouben Mamoulian, to the cast, headed by Alfred Drake, Joan Roberts, a relatively unknown actress-singer named Celeste Holm, and a company of ballet-trained dancers unlike any that had appeared on the Broadway stage before.

LEFT: The second act of the show opened with a barn dance, choreographed by de Mille and led by the exuberant Joan McCracken and Marc Platt.

RIGHT: Celeste Holm as Ado Annie, the girl in a "turrible fix" because she "cain't say no."

One Touch of Venus

THE SHOW THAT Marlene Dietrich turned down became Mary Martin's first starring role on Broadway. *One Touch of Venus* is the tale of Venus, a beautiful statue who comes to life when Rodney, a young barber, slips a wedding ring on her finger. Venus is torn between her love for Rodney and the young rich museum director who is also in love with her. Faced with this dilemma, Venus decides to return to statuary. Happily, Rodney ends up with a young woman who looks just like Venus. This Pygmalion legend with a twist was created by composer Kurt Weill and humorists Ogden Nash and S. J. Perelman. Agnes de Mille created fresh and vivid choreography for lead dancer Sono Osato to round out the show.

LEFT: Mary Martin belting out one of the songs in the show.

ABOVE: Cast member Paula Lawrence rehearsing with the creative team.

RIGHT: Rodney (Kenny Baker) carries the statue-come-to-life.

FAR RIGHT: Martin as Venus.

ONE OF THE GREAT moments of the American stage took place when Paul Robeson appeared in the 1943 Theatre Guild production of *Othello*. With a supporting cast that included José Ferrer as Iago and Uta Hagen as Desdemona, this production was the high point of director Margaret Webster's career. (Ferrer claimed that the role of Iago was the greatest he had ever played.) On opening night, Robeson received ten curtain calls, and the awestruck critics, struggling for words to describe the transcendent performance, all agreed that Robeson had been born to play Othello. At nearly 300 perform-ances, this production had the longest run of any revival of *Othello,* past or present.

TOP: Director Margaret Webster in rehearsal with Paul Robeson and José Ferrer.

BOTTOM: Ferrer as a Mephistophelean Iago.

LEFT: A rapturous moment between Othello (Robeson) and his Desdemona (Hagen), the woman he "loved not wisely but too well."

Bloomer Girl

THE 1940s saw a blossoming of musicals based on historic American themes. One of them, *Bloomer Girl*, tells the story of Evalina Applegate, who becomes radicalized by having to wear hoop skirts (which, ironically, are manufactured by her father). In protest, she joins her aunt Amelia ("Dolly"), who favors baggy bloomers and is an advocate for equal rights for women and freedom for slaves. Of course, Evalina falls for a Southern slave owner named Jeff Calhoun, whom she manages to convert. This Civil War concoction was the work of Harold Arlen (music), E. Y. Harburg (lyrics), and Sig Herzig and Fred Saidy (book), all put together by Harburg as director and Agnes de Mille as choreographer. The show opened on October 5, 1944, and was produced by John C. Wilson and Nat Goldstone.

LEFT TOP: Evalina (Celeste Holm) and Dolly (Margaret Douglass) spend a quiet moment in jail.

LEFT BOTTOM: Dooley Wilson as Pompey.

RIGHT: The team: de Mille and Harburg in deep conversation surrounded by (*left to right*) Lemuel Ayres (scene designer), Sig Herzig, Miles White (costume designer), and Fred Saidy.

Ten Little Indians

EVERY SO OFTEN a staged murder mystery captures the fancy of Broadway audiences. Agatha Christie's *Ten Little Indians* represents a prime example of the genre. Ten people are summoned to a remote island off the coast of Devonshire, England. They are each accused by their mysterious host of having murdered someone. Each person, represented by an Indian figurine on the mantel, comes to an ungentle end, and one by one, the figurines mysteriously fall off the fireplace, until only two are left to solve the murders and escape.

Four of the doomed guests (*left to right*): Anthony Kemble Cooper, Halliwell Hobbs, Harry Worth, and Michael Whelan.

No one expected to learn anything about Russian history from the playwright Mae West, but as the star, she gets to pull out all the stops in this fantasy. A group of GIs envision Catherine the Great as an early version of Diamond Lil. When they summon her up, Catherine moves about in her sumptuous palace and hand-picks her male companions.

ABOVE: The peasant Pugacheff (Bernard Hoffman). A case of boils left him with a cross of hair on his chest, which the peasants interpret as a sign that God chose him to lead Russia.

RIGHT: Since Catherine's favorite habitat is her bed, it is imagined as an ornate, gilded bedstead dressed with satin sheets and plush comforters. The only questionable note in this photograph is the book in her hands that she appears to be reading with rapt attention.

Catherine Was Great

I Remember Mama

EVERY SO OFTEN an unabashedly
sentimental show appears on
Broadway that appeals to the softer
side of usually sophisticated audiences.
In 1944, *I Remember Mama,* written
and directed by John Van Druten,
adapted from a book entitled *Mama's
Bank Account,* was such a play. The
story, narrated by a young writer
named Katrin, centers around a San
Francisco family at the turn of the
century struggling to make do on the
meager earnings of Papa. Mama
apportions his wages and always
manages to put away a few pennies in
a bank account for a rainy day, with
the hope that when their Uncle Chris
dies, he will leave them something.
But when he does pass on, they find
out that there is no money for them
and that the bank account is a fiction
created by Mama to give her children
a sense of security. The play, produced
by Rodgers and Hammerstein, also
marked the Broadway debut of Marlon
Brando.

RIGHT: The family at the dinner
table: Dagmar (Carolyn Hummel),
Papa (Richard Bishop), Christine
(Frances Heflin), Katrin (Joan
Tetzel), Nels (Marlon Brando), and
Mama (Mady Christians).

Sadie Thompson

In 1915, Somerset Maugham created Sadie Thompson; the actress Jeanne Eagles brought her to life on the stage in 1922; and in 1944, composer Vernon Duke and lyricist Howard Dietz put her in a musical. Directed by Rouben Mamoulian and produced by A. P. Waxman, *Sadie Thompson* is set in Pago Pago in the South Seas during the rainy season. Sadie, a woman of dubious morality, finds herself in the company of respectable, middle-class, middle-aged people, including a missionary, the Reverend Alfred Davidson. Davidson decides that he will save Sadie and bring her to God. He almost succeeds —until his own lust for her surfaces. He kills himself, and Sadie goes back to her old life.

LEFT: A series of scenes from the show featuring Sadie (June Havoc) with Quartermaster Bates (Walter Burke) and Sergeant O'Hara (James Newell), and O'Hara with dancing girls.

RIGHT: Sadie (June Havoc) with her admirer, Sergeant O'Hara (James Newell).

Seven Lively Arts

"I LOVED TO PHOTOGRAPH BEA LILLIE," Eileen Darby said, "because she was so nice to be around."
Here, Darby photographed Lillie in *Seven Lively Arts,* a hodgepodge revue produced by showman
Billy Rose at his Ziegfeld Theatre that opened on December 7, 1944. Lillie was paired with the
great clown Bert Lahr, and together they brought down the house in sketches written by Moss Hart,
George S. Kaufman, and Ben Hecht, among others. Cole Porter provided the music.

FAR LEFT: Lillie wore elegant gowns in many of her skits, which contrasted with her uninhibited
antics. Here she is singing Cole Porter's "When I Was a Little Cuckoo."

BOTTOM LEFT: Lillie and Anton Dolin in rehearsal.

ABOVE: "Fragonard in Pink," a big production number with Lahr and Lillie surrounded by a
bevy of chorus girls. Lahr's slapstick comedy was in sharp contrast to his costume and surroundings.

On the Town

EILEEN DARBY WAS LUCKY enough to get the assignment to shoot the production of a new musical by four immensely talented newcomers who would rewrite the history of the musical on Broadway: composer Leonard Bernstein, book writers and lyricists Betty Comden and Adolph Greene, and choreographer Jerome Robbins. *On the Town,* the story of three sailors on twenty-four-hour leave in New York City, was directed by veteran George Abbott and opened on December 29, 1944. Lewis Nichols of the *New York Times* wrote, "*On the Town* is a perfect example of what a well-knit fusion of the respectable arts can provide for the theatre."

In this unusual candid photograph, Adolph Greene, Leonard Bernstein, Paul Feigay (coproducer), and Betty Comden join to sing one of their own songs from the show.

ON THE TOWN grew out of "Fancy Free," a ballet about three sailors on a twenty-four-hour leave in New York. Choreographed by Jerome Robbins, the show was his first work on Broadway. Fleshed out with music by Leonard Bernstein and book and lyrics by Adolph Green and Betty Comden, it became a hit in a decade of hits in the 1940s. A truly integrated work, the dances propelled the story line, a technique that Robbins used again and again in his Broadway career. The young sailors are looking for one thing—girls, of course. One of them, Gaby (John Battles), falls in

love with a picture of Miss Subways (Sono Osato) and tries to find her. (He succeeds.) Ozzie (Adolph Green) falls for Claire de Loon (Betty Comden), an anthropology student. Chip (Cris Alexander) meets Hildy, a cab driver, who tells him that she can cook, but her cuisine is limited to a peeled banana. All three pairs have adventures that take them all around New York.

ABOVE: Claire (Comden) and Ozzie (Green) singing "I Get Carried Away" in the Museum of Natural History.

RIGHT: Nancy Walker backstage.

REPUTED TO BE Richard Rodgers's favorite musical from his and Oscar Hammerstein's pen, *Carousel* took up residence at the Majestic Theatre on April 19, 1945. Based on Ferenc Molnar's play *Lillion, Carousel* is a bittersweet love story between Billy Bigelow, a carnival barker, and Julie Jordan, a simple factory girl. Choreographer Agnes de Mille was unhappy with Rodgers's insistence on having a real carousel on stage, as it left no room for her dancers.

LEFT: Billy Bigelow (John Raitt) and Julie Jordan (Jan Clayton) have eyes only for each other.

ABOVE: Billy (Raitt) and Julie (Clayton) at the carousel.

LEFT: Whenever she could, Darby took photographs of the rehearsals. In this shot, the principals in *Carousel* receive direction from Rouben Mamoulian, who also directed *Oklahoma!*

ABOVE: Louise (Bambi Linn), the daughter of Carrie Pipperidge and Billy Bigelow, feels rejected by the respectable folk she is facing in this picture, much like her father in his dealings with the outside world. Agnes de Mille built a ballet around the unhappy Louise.

Hamlet

MAURICE EVANS first played *Hamlet* on Broadway in 1938. He revived it in 1939 in an uncut version, then in the early 1940s he shortened the play for GI audiences, taking many liberties with the text. The speech to the players became a rehearsal of Agatha Christie's *The Mousetrap*, and the death and burial of Ophelia were eliminated along with the grave diggers' scene. As Major Evans, he toured this *Hamlet* to the armed forces in the South Pacific, then brought it to Broadway on December 13, 1945, under the auspices of Michael Todd.

ABOVE: Evans as Hamlet plotting with his friend Horatio, played by Walter Coy.

Henry IV: *Parts* I *and* II

In 1946, with World War II barely over, Laurence Olivier, at the helm of the Old Vic Repertory Company in London, took his troupe to New York for a limited engagement under the sponsorship of Theatre Incorporated, managed by producer Richard Aldrich. During the month of May, New Yorkers were treated to Shakespeare's *Henry IV,* Parts I and II; Chekhov's *Uncle Vanya; Sophocles, Oedipus Rex,* and Sheridan's *The Critic*. Pictured here are two of the troupe that made the journey.

LEFT: Margaret Leighton as Lady Percy. One of Darby's pictures of Leighton landed on the cover of *Life* magazine for May 6, 1946.

RIGHT: Ralph Richardson made the role of Sir John Falstaff his own, playing in both parts of *Henry IV*. Some critics said that he was the greatest Falstaff that they had ever seen.

Oedipus

"ONE OF MY MOST treasured
assignments was flying off to
London in 1946 to photograph
the Old Vic productions
prior to their arrival in New
York," Darby recalled. "The
productions were wonderful
and I enjoyed photographing
them, particularly Laurence
Olivier in *Oedipus*. The scene
in which Oedipus reappears
on stage after he gouges out
his eyes always brought a
gasp from the audience—from
me, too. I asked him whether
I could take a picture of him
in this scene. Although he
wouldn't pose for it, he gave
me permission to shoot from
the wings with ambient light,
which I did. It doesn't do
justice to his amazing makeup,
but it was the best I could do."

ABOVE LEFT: The
photographer herself caught
in an uncharacteristically
quiet pose.

BELOW LEFT: Oedipus
(Olivier) after he has blinded
himself.

RIGHT: Olivier ready to
go on stage.

The Barretts of Wimpole Street

AFTER KATHARINE CORNELL bought the rights to Rudolph Besier's *The Barretts of Wimpole Street,* she learned that twenty-seven producers had turned it down. For her, it was the role of a lifetime, seemingly written for her, but at first reading, she thought the poet Elizabeth Barrett was an unexciting woman. This 1945 revival, directed by Guthrie McClintic and produced by Cornell herself, reunited her with Brian Aherne and Brenda Forbes from the original 1931 cast and was a triumph for the actress and the company. She took the play on an American tour, then went on to present it to military camps in Europe during World War II.

ABOVE: Robert Browning (Brian Aherne) and Elizabeth Barrett (Katharine Cornell).

Pygmalion

In *Pygmalion*, George Bernard Shaw puts a twist on the ancient myth of Pygmalion, who hates all women until he creates and falls in love with a statue of Galatea, who is brought to life by Aphrodite and becomes Pygmalion's wife. Here, Shaw's Pygmalion, Professor Henry Higgins, transforms Eliza Doolittle, a cockney flower seller, into a lady, passing her off as a duchess at a ball, and eventually falls in love with her. However, unlike the myth, there is no happy ending—Higgins does not marry Eliza. This 1945 revival starred Raymond Massey as Henry Higgins and Gertrude Lawrence as Eliza Doolittle, was produced by Theatre Incorporated (whose managing director, Richard Aldrich, was also, incidentally, Lawrence's husband), and was directed by Cedric Hardwicke.

Left: Professor Higgins (Raymond Massey) gives Eliza (Gertrude Lawrence) her a debut as a "lady" at a tea in his mother's house.

O Mistress Mine

O MISTRESS MINE, with its title taken from Shakespeare, was simply a stage vehicle for the considerable talents of Alfred Lunt and Lynn Fontanne. Although Terence Ratigan was given credit as the author, Lunt's ongoing tinkering with the dialogue and play, which he also directed, made him the de facto playwright. It opened on January 24, 1946, and the loyal followers of the Lunts kept it running both on Broadway and on tour for several years.

ABOVE: Lynn Fontanne as Olivia Brown, the mistress of Sir John Fletcher (Alfred Lunt), an important British Cabinet Minister.

THE 1946 ADAPTATION of Moliere's *Would-be Gentleman* (*Le Bourgeois Gentilhomme*) had all the elements for success, from producer Mike Todd to comic genius Bobby Clark in the starring role, but nothing seemed to work. The story, about a rich bourgeois who hires instructors to teach him how to dance, dress, and act like a gentleman, certainly lent itself to Clark's kind of farce, but audiences did not materialize. The show closed after nine weeks.

BELOW: Clark as the would-be-gentleman getting instruction in the way to dress.

Three to Make Ready

IN 1946, after a half century of success, the revue, as a theatrical form, was in its death throes. That fact did not stop Nancy Hamilton, the creator of a series that began with *One for the Money* (1939), continued with *Two for the Show* (1940), and ended with *Three to Make Ready* in 1946. The cast was brimming with talent, including Bibi Osterwald, Gordon MacRae, Harold Lang, and Carleton Carpenter, but the undisputed star was Ray Bolger (*above*), whose amazing dancing and comedic acting saved the show from lapsing into the ordinary.

GARSON KANIN's comedy *Born Yesterday* had a long trip to Broadway. Producer Max Gordon took an option on the play, sent Kanin a contract, and waited and waited while Kanin fulfilled other commitments. Paul Douglas was signed to play Harry Brock, the king of the junkyards, who pays off a senator to watch over his interests. With him in his expensive and garish Washington hotel suite is his mistress Billie Dawn, who is in want of a finishing school to smooth the rough edges, clean up her grammar, and generally make her presentable to the junk king's Washington associates. The "finishing school" turns out

to be Paul Verrall, a handsome young journalist from the *New Republic,* played by Gary Merrill. He introduces Billie to books and ideas and awakens her mind, which both of them discover is very good. She also realizes that the man she has been living with is up to his ears in illegal activities. Inevitably, Billie and Paul fall in love and threaten to expose Harry.

Movie star Jean Arthur seemed ideal and was signed to play the part, but she created so many problems that Gordon fired her shortly before the play opened. Out of the blue came Judy Holliday, who made the part her own. The show opened on February 4, 1946, to rave reviews. It was a huge hit and made Judy Holliday a star.

LEFT: Billie Dawn (Holliday) and Harry Brock (Douglas).

RIGHT: Billie getting her lesson from Paul (Gary Merrill).

ABOVE: Playwright and director Garson Kanin; producer Max Gordon; and Kanin's wife, Ruth Gordon.

Born Yesterday

Present Laughter

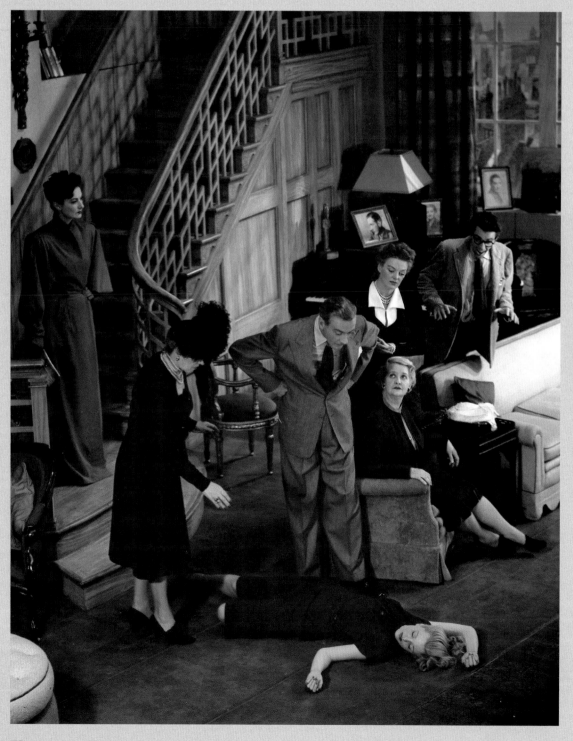

EILEEN DARBY was very busy in the 1940s on Broadway. There were musicals, revivals, plays, farces—and Noel Coward. Darby photographed several of Coward's plays during this time, among them *Present Laughter*. As usual, the plot was as thin as a gossamer thread, the dialogue sparkling and witty. Coward's not-so-polite comedy centers around Garry Essendine, a philandering husband, who delights in seducing other women, including his best friend's wife. In typical Coward fashion, at the end of the play Essendine abandons his wicked ways and returns to his tolerant wife.

LEFT: Essendine (Clifton Webb) contemplates one of his girlfriends, who faints dead away when she is informed of his infidelities.

RIGHT: Clifton Webb is caught in the act of changing costumes backstage.

Happy Birthday

"THROUGH THESE PORTALS pass the nicest people in Newark" proclaims the sign above the archway of the Jersey Mecca Cocktail Bar in *Happy Birthday,* a comedy by Anita Loos. Through those portals also passes Addie Bemis, a meek and repressed librarian in pursuit of Paul, for whom she has a secret passion. Before he arrives, she experiments with the devil's brew. Four pink ladies and a double scotch later, a drunk Addie loses her inhibitions and gets her man. The show, which opened in October 1946, was produced by Rodgers and Hammerstein, who also wrote the few featured songs.

LEFT: Addie (Helen Hayes) sits primly at the bar before it begins to shake and shimmer after she imbibes her cocktails.

RIGHT: Addie takes to the dance floor in a tango.

Cyrano de Bergerac

CONSIDERED a tour de force, the part of Cyrano has been played many times by many actors. The actor Walter Hampden had almost a monopoly on the part, first playing Cyrano in 1923 and reviving it in 1926, 1928, 1932, and 1936. José Ferrer scored a triumph when he produced and starred in this 1946 version of Rostand's play adapted by Brian Hooker. Ferrer surrounded himself with an able cast that included Frances Reid as the beauteous Roxane and Ernest Graves as the shy and tongue-tied Christian who asks Cyrano to be his unseen surrogate lover to Roxane. Levity was provided by Hiram Sherman as the poet/pastry-cook and Paula Lawrence as Roxane's Duenna.

LEFT: Ferrer displays the extraordinary Cyrano nose.

RIGHT: The pop singer and future Mrs. Ferrer, Rosemary Clooney, looks on admiringly as José begins his makeup in his dressing room.

ABOVE LEFT: *Life* magazine commissioned Eileen Darby to take backstage pictures of how Ferrer accomplished the awesome feat of building the famous Cyrano nose. Here, Ferrer putting the finishing touches on his makeup.

BELOW LEFT AND FACING PAGE: Roxane's Duenna (Paula Lawrence) in a playful vignette with Cyrano (José Ferrer).

IN 1946, English poet W. H. Auden adapted John Webster's *The Duchess of Malfi* for modern audiences. This Shakespearean-era tragedy depicts a family that destroys itself because of the perception by the brothers of the Duchess of Malfi that she is leading an adulterous life and ruining the family honor. The brothers plant a spy in her household to find a reason to murder her and her children so they can take over her domain and preserve the good name of the family. By the final curtain, all nine of the principal characters have perished either by murder or execution.

LEFT: The Duchess (Elisabeth Bergner) is strangled by her brothers' henchmen.

The Duchess of Malfi

No Exit

JOHN-PAUL SARTRE'S 1946 PLAY, *No Exit,* grew out of the author's postwar despair and his evolving philosophy that came to be known as Existentialism. The play, directed by John Huston, takes place in hell, where three characters are locked in the fate they created for themselves in life: Cradeau, a collaborator, a coward, and, perhaps, a wife-beater; Inez, a lesbian who destroyed the life of a married woman with whom she was in love; and Estelle, who betrayed her husband. Each looks to the other for understanding and salvation, but each is too egocentric to believe that his or her doom is self-made.

Estelle (Ruth Ford), Cradeau (Claude Dauphin), and Inez (Annabella).

Finian's Rainbow

So ROOTED in its times is *Finian's Rainbow* that there is very little likelihood it will ever be revived in a full-scale Broadway production. The satire on the state of affairs in America in 1947 took aim at the economic system, social injustice, and racism with a fantasy about an Irish immigrant named Finian McLonergan going to Rainbow Valley, Missitucky, to bury a stolen crock of gold (read Fort Knox) and watch it grow and make him rich. It also involves a bigoted senator named Billboard Rawkins who is taught a lesson by being transformed into a black man by a leprechaun. Written by E. Y. Harburg and Fred Saidy, with music by Burton Lane and directed by Bretaigne Windust, *Finian's Rainbow* opened on January 10, 1947, to great acclaim.

LEFT: David Wayne as Og the leprechaun, who sings about his love for all girls.

ABOVE: A ballet created by choreographer Michael Kidd.

RIGHT: Finian (Albert Sharpe), his daughter, Sharon (Ella Logan), and her paramour, labor organizer Woody Mahoney (Donald Richards).

The Importance of Being Earnest

THE THEATRE GUILD'S 1947 production of Oscar Wilde's *The Importance of Being Earnest,* directed by and starring John Gielgud, with its veddy proper British cast, had a *New York Times* reviewer note "how the actors held their heads high as though they were elevating themselves above vulgarity." The plot, a send-up of the typical nineteenth-century poor-child-is-actually-a-noble dramas, has a Wilde twist: here the hero finds out that he was really named Ernest, a name preferred by his lady.

ABOVE: Lady Bracknell (Margaret Rutherford, center) is cosseted by Jack (John Gielgud) and Gwendolyn (Pamela Brown), while Algernon (Robert Flemyng) and Cecily (Jane Baxter) kiss.

LEFT: Jack and his best friend, Algernon.

FAR LEFT: Jack announces to his friends that his imaginary brother "Ernest" has just died.

High Button Shoes

FOR MANY YEARS, if a casting director looked for an actor who could convincingly portray a con man, the choice would inevitably have been Phil Silvers. On Broadway, on television, and in movies, Silvers played the quintessential con man to perfection but always with humor and style. As Harrison Floy, in the 1947 musical *High Button Shoes,* he returns to his hometown of New Brunswick, New Jersey, in 1913 and tries a number of ploys to take money from his erstwhile neighbors. He sells worthless land belonging to the Longstreets and loses the ill-gained profits by betting on the wrong football team. The show, written by George Abbott (assisted by Silvers), directed by Abbott, and choreographed by Jerome Robbins, also marked Jule Styne's debut on Broadway as a composer, working with lyricist Sammy Cahn.

LEFT: The stars: Phil Silvers and Nanette Fabray.

RIGHT: Harrison with his sidekick Pontdue (Joey Faye), hawking fraudulent wares.

A Streetcar Named Desire

The original production of Tennessee Williams's play *A Streetcar Named Desire* is a perfect example of the best in the American theater. The combination of a superb cast and a wonderful script made this production a memorable event when it debuted at the Ethel Barrymore Theatre on December 3, 1947. The critics could find no weak element in the show—Elia Kazan's direction and Jo Mielziner's claustrophobic set and lighting were perfect for the unfolding drama. *Streetcar* established Williams as the leading playwright in America and has since been translated and produced all over the world. Eileen Darby's photographs were also widely published and have become the icons of the play.

Left: Blanche (Jessica Tandy) shown here in her finery as her mind begins to slide toward insanity. The role of Blanche was such a triumph for Tandy that it became the benchmark for all the actresses who assayed the part after her and established her once and for all as one of the great players of the English-speaking stage.

Right: Darby caught the playwright as an enigma: the sidelong glance, open shirt, and cigarette in hand imbued Tennessee Williams with a mysterious and slightly dangerous persona.

LEFT: From the moment Blanche (Jessica Tandy) steps into the seedy apartment shared by her sister Stella (Kim Hunter) and her brutish husband, Stanley (Marlon Brando), there is a sense that the characters are on a collision course. Although Stella attempts to shield Blanche from Stanley's resentment, he is never to be placated. In the searing climactic scene, he confronts Blanche with her past and her tissue of lies. He tells her, as he brutally attacks her: "We've had this date with each other from the beginning."

ABOVE: Just as Mitch (Karl Malden) rejects Blanche and exposes the lies about her past, a Mexican woman appears at the door selling "flowers for the dead." Blanche regards the woman as the messenger of her doom and waves her away. Darby's composition of this photograph reveals the full poignancy of the scene as Mitch watches Blanche begin her descent into insanity by recalling episodes from her life in a stream of consciousness.

Williams contemplated titling his play *The Poker Game* but wisely decided on the final title. The idea of the poker game as a metaphor for life resonates throughout the play: in life as in the game, there are winners and losers, there are risk takers and safe bettors; and finally, the game begins again and never ends.

BELOW: This scene, which Williams called "The Poker Night,"

comes early in the play when Blanche (Jessica Tandy) meets Mitch (Karl Malden) for the first time.

RIGHT: Darby brilliantly captures the emotional final scene, which takes place against the background of another game of poker. Mitch hides his head in his arms at the poker table, and Stanley embraces and comforts Stella (*far left*) as Blanche is led gently into the shadows on the arm of the doctor from the state institution, uttering the now famous and strangely ironic line, "I have always depended on the kindness of strangers."

Where's Charley?

THE ENTIRE COMIC PREMISE of *Where's Charley?* is in the decision of Oxford undergraduates Charley Wykeham and Jack Chesney to pretend that one of them is an old aunt so they can entertain their lady loves Amy and Kitty in their own rooms without a chaperone. All of the fun flows from the complications that this prank causes—until the real aunt shows up. The book by George Abbott (who also directed) was derived from Brandon Thomas's 1882 farce, *Charley's Aunt*. Produced by Cy Feuer and Ernest Martin and choreographed by George Balanchine, it opened on October 11, 1948, and marked composer-lyricist Frank Loesser's Broadway debut.

ABOVE: Charley (Ray Bolger) as his own aunt in full Victorian regalia, surrounded by a bevy of beautiful ladies.

Inside

U.S.A.

ABOUT THE ONLY THING taken from John Gunther's bestselling social commentary *Inside U.S.A.* was the title. Howard Dietz and Arthur Schwartz's 1948 musical revue brought Beatrice Lillie and Jack Haley back to Broadway, supported by a cast that eventually gained television fame: Carl Reiner, Louis Nye, Herb Shriner, and Jack Cassidy. Each sketch had a different setting, from Jackson Hole, Wyoming; Chilicothe, Ohio; Pittsburgh; Miami Beach; New Orleans; and Albuquerque to, of course, New York City.

ABOVE LEFT: In the Chicago sketch: Eric Victor as Doctor Zilmore, Carl Reiner as the Judge, and Valerie Bettis as Tiger Lily, the gun moll.

TOP RIGHT: Bea Lillie as the Massachusetts Mermaid.

ABOVE RIGHT: Bea Lillie and Jack Haley in rehearsal.

SUMMER AND SMOKE was the third Tennessee Williams play Darby photographed and it would not be her last. The 1948 play premiered on the heels of the brilliant success of *A Streetcar Named Desire* and was, of course, compared to it; Jo Mielziner's sets again received rave reviews, but the show did not fare as well. Alma Winemiller, the play's heroine, was Williams's favorite character, but as the critics pointed out, she was a copy of Blanche from *Streetcar*.

TOP LEFT: Alma Winemiller (Margaret Phillips) is both attracted to and repelled by the young Dr. Buchanan (Todd Andrews), her next-door neighbor.

LEFT: The young doctor eventually falls in love with Nellie Ewell (Anne Jackson).

TOP RIGHT: The elder Dr. Buchanan (Ralph Theadore) wields a stick at Papa Gonzales (Sid Cassel) and Rosa Gonzales (Monica Boyer).

RIGHT: Jo Mielziner's set dominates this scene between Dr. Buchanan (Andrews) and Alma (Phillips).

Summer and Smoke

Kiss Me, Kate

THE FERTILE MUSICAL BRAIN of Cole Porter was put to a challenge by his collaborators Sam and Bella Spewack, who fashioned a book of a play within a play. The backstage marital battle between an actor and his ex-wife mirrors Petruchio and Kate, the characters they are portraying in Shakespeare's *Taming of the Shrew*. A secondary and equally rocky romance between the saucy Bianca and the gambling Bill provides a counterpoint to the main plot. The shifts between reality and stage illusion in the book are complemented by Cole Porter's magnificent score, which does the same, with songs such as "It's Too Darn Hot," "So In Love," and "Brush Up Your Shakespeare."

LEFT: Cole Porter at his piano serenading his Skipperke dog.

ABOVE: The troupe in costume during a rehearsal break.

LEFT: In this scene, Lois Lane (Lisa Kirk) berates her lover, Bill Calhoun (Harold Lang), in Cole Porter's song "Why Can't You Behave?" Porter's lyrics were clever, sophisticated, and witty, and sometimes, to quote critic Brooks Atkinson of the *New York Times*, "they would shock the editorial staff of *The Police Gazette*."

RIGHT: Another of his delightful songs was "Brush Up Your Shakespeare" in which two thugs (Jack Diamond and Harry Clarke) advise that quoting the Bard will so impress women that "they will all kowtow."

ABOVE: Darby's shot of the full stage reveals as much of the scenery and costumes as was possible to achieve. The only regret is that it was not captured in color. All the production elements were the work of one designer, Lemuel Ayres, who spared no expense in giving the show colorful and artful scenery and beautiful costumes and who also wore another hat as one of the producers. The musical ran for more than one thousand performances and gave added luster to the name of Cole Porter.

Death of a Salesman

Darby captured the full impact of Jo Mielziner's inspired set for *Death of a Salesman* in this wide-angle photograph (*right*). Seated at the table are Willy Loman (Lee J. Cobb) and his wife, Linda (Mildred Dunnock). Above them in the bedroom are their two sons, Biff (Arthur Kennedy) and Happy (Cameron Mitchell). Using lighting and scrim curtains, Mielziner was able to create plausible flashbacks. The director Elia Kazan once told Mielziner that the set directed the play, not he.

Above: Linda's (Dunnock) concern for her husband (Cobb) is palpable in this picture.

Eileen Darby confessed an inability to understand Arthur Miller's *Death of a Salesman*. Willy Loman's unfulfilled dreams and wasted life, his tortured relationship with his wife and sons, and his eventual and inevitable breakdown were too foreign to her own experience. Her photographs, however, give no indication of her confusion and bring to life the unfolding tragedy. The play won many awards for Miller, including the 1949 Pulitzer Prize.

LEFT TOP: Producer Kermit Bloomgarden, director Elia Kazan, coproducer Walter Fried, and playwright Arthur Miller.

LEFT: In another flashback, Willy's brother Ben (Thomas Chalmers) appears as if in a dream and displays his prowess as a fighter. He pins the younger and stronger Biff (Kennedy) and tells him, "Never fight fair with a stranger."

RIGHT: A reconciliation of sorts between Willy and his sons.

BELOW: Linda at Willy's grave still not understanding the reason for Willy's suicide, surrounded by (*left to right*) Bernard (Don Keefer), Charlie, Biff, and Happy.

WHEN *The Member of the Wedding* had its pre-Broadway tryout in Philadelphia in 1950, the local critics predicted that it would receive favorable reviews but close in a week. They were almost right. It *did* receive excellent reviews, but it went on to run for 501 performances—nearly sixty-one weeks. Although the play had no structure and the slimmest of plots, the acting was superb. Twenty-five-year-old Julie Harris is the twelve-year-old tomboy Frankie, whose best friends are the housekeeper, Berenice, played by the legendary actress-singer Ethel Waters, and young John Henry, played by seven-and-a-half-year-old Brandon de Wilde, who gave a thoroughly disarming performance without a hint of child-actor precocity.

LEFT: Frankie (Julie Harris) and John Henry (Brandon de Wilde) in the seedy kitchen where all the action takes place.

ABOVE: Frankie (Harris), in a belligerent mood, confronts Berenice (Ethel Waters).

RIGHT: Berenice (Waters) enjoys a rare moment of levity.

Gentlemen Prefer Blondes

CAROL CHANNING BECAME a star as the gold-digging flapper Lorelei Lee, the little girl from Little Rock whose best friends are diamonds, in *Gentlemen Prefer Blondes,* the 1949 musical version of a successful novel and play written by Anita Loos in 1926. Lorelei, accompanied by her friend Dorothy, runs through the male population aboard a cruise ship, making conquests and acquiring a diamond tiara from her admirer, Sir Francis Beekman, while Dorothy acquires a husband.

Lorelei (Channing) and her daddy (who "ain't her Pa"), Sir Frances (Rex Evans).

THE STORY of Sally Adams, a brash American hostess who becomes Ambassador to the mythical country Lichtenburg and blusters her way through European traditions, was inspired by Perle Mesta, a Washington party giver appointed by President Truman as Ambassador to Luxembourg. Sally's no-nonsense manner charms the Prime Minister, while her aide, Kenneth Gibson, falls in love with Lichtenburg's Princess Marie.

BELOW: The production team including director George Abbott (kneeling) and composer Irving Berlin with their star.

RIGHT: La Merman as Sally Adams in a Mainbocher gown.

As You Like It

In the 1950 revival of Shakespeare's *As You Like It,* Katharine Hepburn showed off her versatility as an actress as well as her much heralded legs. The *New York Times* critic, however, reluctantly stated: "There is too much Yankee in Miss Hepburn for Shakespeare's glades and lyric fancies." As Rosalind, the moonstruck maiden who follows her lover, Orlando (William Prince), into the Forest of Arden to test the depth of his emotions, Hepburn looked beautiful but her personality was simply too overpowering. Michael Benthall directed, the Theatre Guild produced, and James Bailey provided the lush scenery and exquisite costumes.

ABOVE: Rosalind as she finally appears in women's clothes at the conclusion of the play.

RIGHT: Hepburn enjoys a cigarette in the wings before she and William Prince (seated) go on stage.

Guys and Dolls

RIGHT: EILEEN DARBY's stop-action photograph of a crap game in a sewer captures the intensity of the assembled gamblers as they watch Sky Masterson (Robert Alda) throw the dice. What looks like solid scenery is actually a painted drop curtain designed by Jo Mielziner, but Darby's photograph gives little hint of what it really is. Choreographer Michael Kidd staged a boisterous dance in the sewer scene, certainly one of the unlikeliest backgrounds for a ballet.

ABOVE: Also unlikely was the romance between Sky and Salvation Army lass Sarah Brown (Isabel Bigley), who tries to reform Sky and his gang of miscreants. The 1950 musical, written by Frank Loesser and directed by George S. Kaufman, was a huge hit.

The King and I

IT WAS GERTRUDE LAWRENCE who suggested to Richard Rodgers and Oscar Hammerstein II making a musical from *Anna and the King of Siam,* a novel about the adventures of the real Anna Leonowens. The role was tailored for Lawrence, but her unknown costar, Yul Brynner, stole the show as the King. Although John Van Druten was the director, Brynner stepped in and virtually staged it himself. Rodgers and Hammerstein not only wrote the musical, but also produced the show, which opened on March 29, 1951, and went on to have a three-year run.

LEFT: Director John Van Druten and Gertrude Lawrence with two of the King's children.

ABOVE: The King (Brynner), now mortally ill, sends for Anna (Lawrence) and the son who will succeed him.

BELOW: A high point of the show is "The Small House of Uncle Thomas," one of the cleverest ballets ever to appear in a musical, choreographed by Jerome Robbins.

A Tree Grows in Brooklyn

IF EVER a musical had all the ingredients to make a huge hit, *A Tree Grows in Brooklyn* did: a book by George Abbott and Betty Smith (from Smith's bestselling novel); music by Arthur Schwartz and lyrics by Dorothy Fields; choreography by Herbert Ross; set design by Jo Mielziner; and produced and directed by George Abbott. It opened April 19, 1951, and, largely because of Shirley Booth's star power, managed to run 267 performances, only a fraction of the usual run of a hit musical. Perhaps the mixture was too rich for this simple Brooklyn tale of love and marriage set in an Irish neighborhood.

LEFT: Cissy (Shirley Booth) and Harry (Nathaniel Frey) in a playful mood.

RIGHT: Herbert Ross's nightmarish ballet with Johnny Nolan (Johnny Johnston) in the center.

Two on the Aisle

TWO ON THE AISLE (1951) was the last of the great revues—noisy, smart, and funny. The fun was provided by the witty lyrics and music of Betty Comden and Adolph Green, who sent up opera ("Catch Our Act at the Met") and the trope of the jilted lover ("If") in their boffo numbers; the sketches written by Nat Hiken and Abe Burrows; and Bert Lahr, who in the course of one evening got to play a baseball player, a park trash-picker, Queen Victoria, a Wagnerian Siegfried, and, as pictured here, Captain Universe. "He's the freest man I've ever seen on stage," Burrows said of Lahr, who earned a *Time* magazine cover for his clowning in the show. Burrows went on: "Bert has tremendous control. I used to stand in the wings some nights. He'd be in the middle of a scene that wasn't going well. He'd see me standing there and, still in character, stride toward the wings, and say, 'They're from the moose country tonight!' Without missing a beat, he'd go back into the scene."

Gigi

ON NOVEMBER 24, 1951, Broadway welcomed a new star when Audrey Hepburn debuted in *Gigi,* a worldly play about the rite of passage from a lovely young girl into a beautiful woman written by Anita Loos, adapted from a novel by Colette. Dick Maney commissioned Eileen Darby to shoot both the rehearsals and the show. Her pictures capture the charm and unusual beauty of the twenty-two-year-old actress on the brink of a dazzling career on stage and in films.

LEFT: Hepburn as the sixteen-year-old Gigi.

RIGHT: Although her female relatives try to instruct her in the ways of their world, warning her that she must find a rich lover, Gigi resists their admonitions and asks her grandmother why she was not given lessons in dance so that she could have had a career as a dancer. Mme. Alvarez replies: "A career is the ruination of any woman."

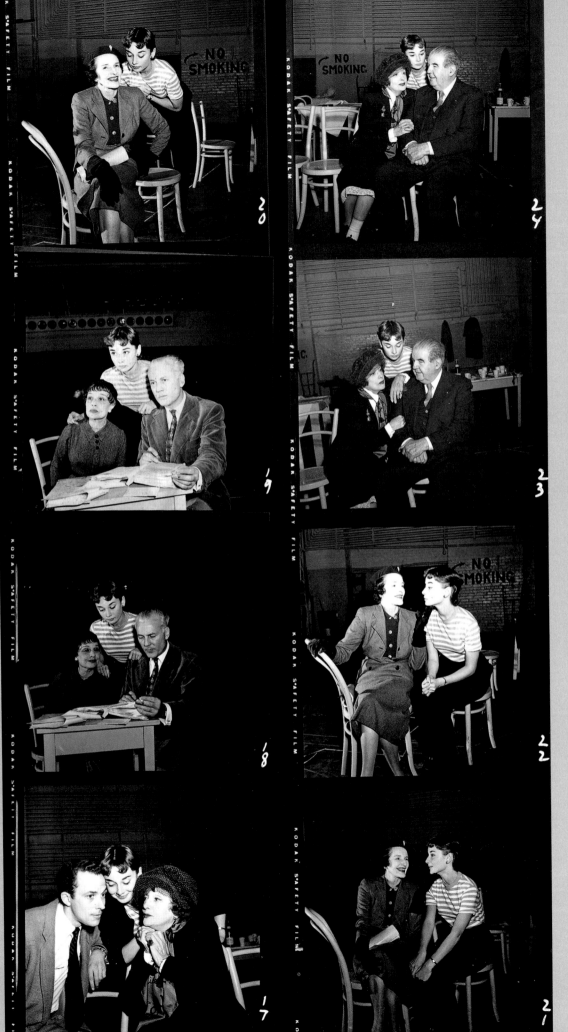

The cast in rehearsal, *top left:* Gigi (Hepburn) and her aunt, Alicia de St. Ephlam (Cathleen Nesbitt); *top right:* Hepburn with Josephine Brown (as her grandmother Mme. Alvarez) and the producer, Gilbert Miller; *second row left:* Hepburn with playwright Anita Loos and director Raymond Rouleau; *second row right:* Hepburn, Brown, and Miller; *third row left:* Hepburn, Loos, and Rouleau; *third row right:* Hepburn and Nesbitt; *bottom left:* Michael Evans (as Gaston Lachaille), Hepburn, and Brown; *bottom row right:* Hepburn and Nesbitt.

RIGHT: Gaston, a rich young bachelor and a family friend, who has been deceived by his mistress, enters their flat with gifts of candy for Gigi, with whom he plays cards. When, at the end of the play, he realizes that he has fallen in love with Gigi and asks for her hand in marriage, Mme. Alvarez is stunned. Gigi confesses her love for Gaston, and her family gets used to respectability for their young charge.

Pal Joey

IN 1940, the writer John O'Hara created the first true
Broadway antihero and Rodgers and Hart put him in a
musical. *Pal Joey,* the story of a charming, talented, class-A
heel whose cushy arrangement with a rich widow is
threatened by a goody-two-shoes chorus girl, was not fully
comprehended by critics or audiences when it opened on
Broadway, but twelve years later, it was revived to great
acclaim. In 1940, the *New York Times* critic Brooks
Atkinson called the story "a drab and mirthless world of
punk's progress," but in 1952 he found much to admire in
the musical. *Pal Joey* did not come of age—its audiences did.
In this 1952 revival, Harold Lang is Joey, the role Gene Kelly
originated on Broadway. The scenes set in the cabaret gave
Robert Alton, the choreographer of both versions, many
opportunities for staging spectacular dances.

FAR LEFT: Barbara Nichols as a cabaret performer.

ABOVE: One of the ballets created by Alton and David
Alexander.

LEFT: Harold Lang and Helen Wood being instructed
by Alton.

RIGHT: Harold Lang and Helen Gallagher enjoy a respite
during the rehearsal.

Vivienne Segal reprises the role of Vera, who becomes "bewitched, bothered, and bewildered" by Joey in this 1952 revival. Eventually Vera loses her patience and her passion and cuts Joey loose; predictably, he goes back to his old ways. In another step on her way to stardom, Elaine Stritch as Melba Snyder stopped the show with her rendition of "Zip," a song about what goes through a stripper's mind as she disrobes. The original production also helped the careers of Gene Kelly, Van Johnson, Stanley Donen, and June Havoc.

LEFT: Darby catches Lang (and his shadow) in a sensational leap.

RIGHT: Elaine Stritch (*left*), Vivienne Segal, and Harold Lang in an early rehearsal.

An Evening with Bea Lillie

BEATRICE LILLIE'S evening was a long one. The show, which consisted of a series of sketches (in which she was the centerpiece), began in July 1952 as a summer theater tour, then moved to Broadway in October and ran nearly three hundred performances before it went on the road in the United States and Canada for another year. She then took the show to England, appearing first in Liverpool before opening in London on November 4, 1954. Then it was off to the English provinces until it was time to return to America for another tour. In the end, Beatrice Lillie's evening lasted more than four years.

LEFT: In her signature pillbox hat and elegant gown, Lillie appears with a drawing of herself on a full-sized drop curtain.

TOP RIGHT: Lillie accompanying herself on "The Zither Song."

RIGHT: Costar Reginald Gardiner in "The Conductor" sketch.

*Two's
Company*

OLD SOLDIERS may just fade away, but old Hollywood stars go back to Broadway, where most of them started. In 1952, Bette Davis returned as the star of the revue *Two's Company*. Directed by John Murray Anderson, choreographed by Jerome Robbins, and with music by Vernon Duke set to lyrics by Ogden Nash, Bette was in very good company. She appeared in six of the sketches as everything from a glamorous, hot-blooded actress in Rome to a hillbilly singer. According to the critics, she was not a success in all of them, but she certainly was game.

CLOCKWISE FROM UPPER LEFT: Davis as Tallulah Bankhead breaking up a Bette Davis film premiere; as the vamp Sadie Thompson; and as a kitchen slattern, with David Burns, in a sketch entitled "Jealousy."

WHEN *The Children's Hour,* written by Lillian Hellman, first appeared on Broadway in 1934, it shocked audiences with the *implication* that two women (or at least one of them) had an "unnatural affection" for each other. When producer Kermit Bloomgarden revived the play in 1952, that shock had worn off, but the play still told a tragic story about two headmistresses of a private school whose lives are shattered by childish malevolence and the power of an insidious rumor, resulting in the suicide of the one who may indeed have been in love with her friend.

LEFT: Mary (Iris Mann) and grandmother (Katherine Emmet).

*The
Children's Hour*

John Brown's Body

IN 1953, the actor Charles Laughton adapted Stephen Vincent Benét's long poem "John Brown's Body" into a dramatized reading. The poem, about the abolitionist John Brown, who almost single-handedly started the Civil War by his acts of terror against slavery and slave owners, gives the entire panorama of the war while Brown's body is "a-moldering in the grave." Laughton also directed the ensemble of actors, singers, and dancers led by Raymond Massey, Tyrone Power, and Judith Anderson, who narrated the piece.

ABOVE: The narrators Raymond Massey, Tyrone Power, and Judith Anderson.

WHEN WRITER Abe Burrows journeyed to Paris to find out whether there was any truth to the accepted fact that the can-can dance was banned in Paris in the 1890s and discovered that there were indeed sanctions against it, it gave him the idea for a musical. *Can-Can*, set in 1890s Paris, is about Forestier, a young judge sent to investigate the charges against Pistache, the proprietress of the Bal du Paradis, where the can-can is performed. He falls in love with her and becomes her champion—and husband.

Meanwhile, Claudine, a can-can dancer, inadvertently causes a hilarious duel to be fought between Boris and his rival Hilaire, an art critic who severely criticizes the artist's work.

LEFT: Claudine (Gwen Verdon) performs the can-can's exuberant high kick.

CENTER: Boris (Hans Conried), the artist who loves Claudine, in his studio with model (Pat Turner).

RIGHT: Lilo (Pistache) and Gwen Verdon during rehearsal.

Can-Can

The last scene of Act I ends with the famed Quatz Arts Ball held annually in Paris. Choreographer Michael Kidd took the Garden of Eden theme and turned the ball into a ballet fantasy. Motley's spectacular costumes were the highlight of the show.

LEFT: Gwen Verdon as Eve being enticed by Snake (Bert May) to partake of the fatal apple.

RIGHT CENTER: Ralph Beaumont and Pat Turner as Leopards.

RIGHT: Ruth Vernon and Tom Panko as Sea Horses.

Me and Juliet

WHEN *Me and Juliet* opened in May 1953, most critics agreed it was not up to typical Rodgers and Hammerstein standards. The book, an original by Oscar Hammerstein, takes a look at backstage life while a show is being presented. It was a challenge for scene designer Jo Mielziner, who had to juxtapose the backstage activity and the onstage performance on the same stage without the audience becoming confused. The musical centers around two couples: Jeanie, a chorus girl, and Larry, the assistant stage manager, who is being stalked by a jealous rival, a heavy-drinking stage electrician; and Betty, a dancer who tries hard to get the attention of Mac, the stage manager to whom she is attracted. He refuses to socialize with the cast, but when he is transferred to another show, their romance blossoms.

LEFT TOP: Designer Jo Mielziner in his studio pondering the difficulties of the scene designs for the show.

LEFT: A scene of the show-within-a-show with the dance ensemble and, at the table, Juliet and Don Juan (Helena Scott and Bob Fortier), the leads in the "show."

ABOVE: Jeanie (Isabel Bigley) and Larry (Bill Hayes).

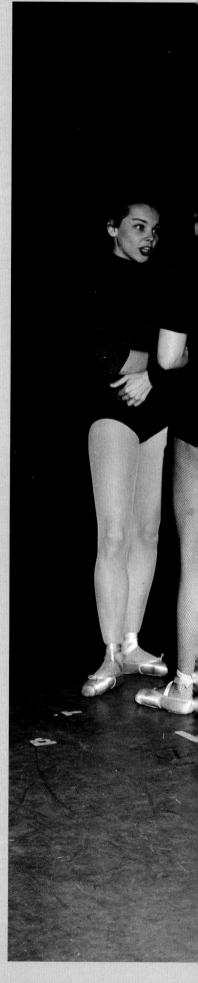

ABOVE: Dancers Arthur
Maxwell, Bob Fortier, and
Joan McCracken.

RIGHT: The chorus girls,
backstage, being given notes.
Chorine Shirley MacLaine is
second from right.

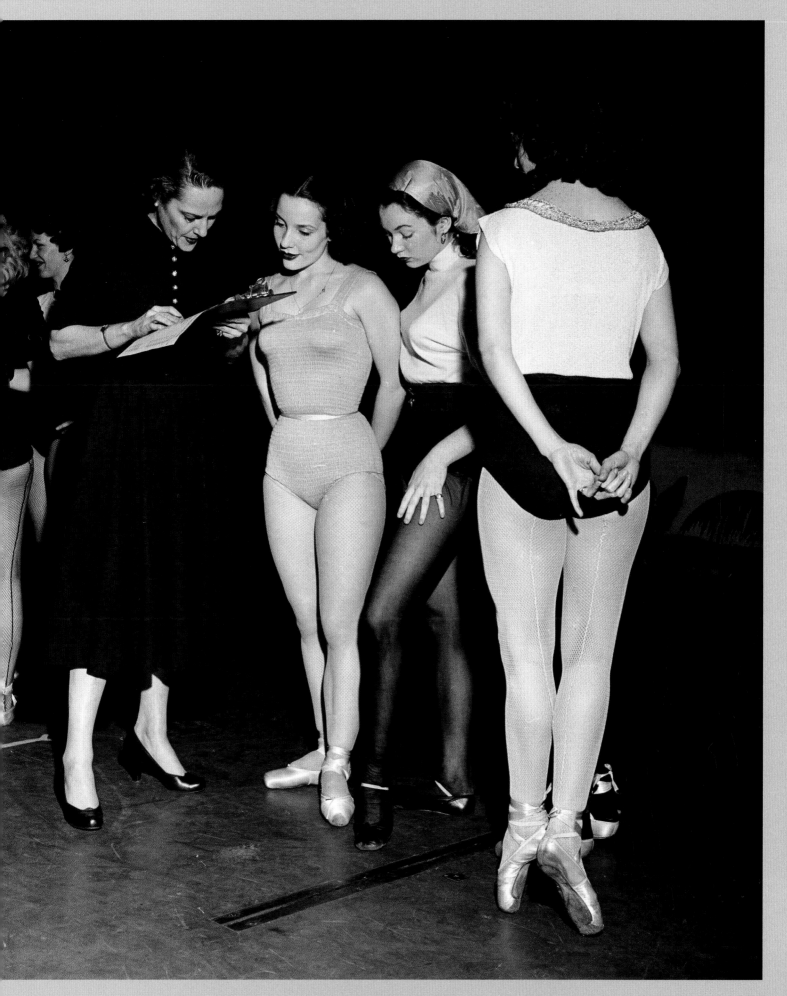

ME AND JULIET was written and produced by Richard Rodgers and Oscar Hammerstein, directed by George Abbott, and choreographed by Robert Alton. The melody of the most popular song of the show, "No Other Love," was originally used by Rodgers as background music for the television series *Victory at Sea*.

OPPOSITE TOP: Stage electricians Sidney (Edwin Phillips) and Bob (Mark Dawson) on the light bridge.

OPPOSITE CENTER: The backstage crew looks up to the flies as the show goes on.

OPPOSITE BOTTOM (*left to right*): Jeanie (Isabel Bigley), Larry (Bill Hayes), Bob (Mark Dawson), Mac (Ray Walston), Ruby (Joe Lautner), and Betty (Joan McCracken).

ABOVE: The onstage dancers under a giant roulette wheel.

The Trip to Bountiful

HORTON FOOTE'S *The Trip to Bountiful* was first seen on the *Philco Hour* in the early days of live television. The story of a lonely Texas widow who longs for the home in Bountiful, where she spent her happiest days, was not a hit when it was produced on Broadway, despite Foote's elegiac script and the shining performance of Lillian Gish as the widow. It opened on November 3, 1953, and closed a month later. Eva Marie Saint had a small but important role as the widow's newfound friend and confidante on the bus back to Bountiful. Her acting so impressed Elia Kazan that he cast her in his film *On the Waterfront.*

LEFT: Mrs. Carrie Watts (Lillian Gish) and her newfound friend Thelma (Eva Marie Saint).

RIGHT: Darby's shot of the magnificent Gish face reveals a mixture of profound sadness and resignation as the widow sits on the steps of her former home.

THE *NEW YORK TIMES* in 1951 described *The Boy Friend* as "a caricature of the hokum musical comedy of the Twenties" and found much to admire in it. The half-English and half-American cast was superb, but the reviewer singled out Julie Andrews in her role as Polly, a poor little rich girl who falls in love with a charming messenger boy, who turns out to be the son of aristocrats. The book, music, and lyrics

all came from the hand of Sandy Wilson, who somehow transformed all the clichés of the era's songs and dances to be humorous but not heavy-handed and overblown.

ABOVE: The girls at Mme. Dubonnet's finishing school with their boyfriends, dancing to the tune "Won't You Charleston with Me?" Polly (Andrews) and Tony (John Hewer) are the first couple on the far left.

The Boy Friend

John Murray Anderson's Almanac

JOHN MURRAY ANDERSON'S *ALMANAC* all but closed the book on the revue but proved that there was still life in the form. In 1953, Anderson assembled a cast including Hermione Gingold, Billy De Wolfe, Harry Belafonte, Orson Bean, Polly Bergen, and Carleton Carpenter that gave the audience its money's worth. Sketches were provided by seasoned writers and directed by Cyril Ritchard, and a new Broadway team of Richard Adler and Jerry Ross (*Pajama Game, Damn Yankees*) provided most of the songs and lyrics. A very young Belafonte thrilled the audiences with his rendition of "Hold 'em Joe," which became part of his repertoire, but it was the comic antics of Gingold and De Wolfe that stopped the show.

TOP: Harry Belafonte.

RIGHT: Hermione Gingold and Billy De Wolfe (in drag) as Mrs. A and Mrs. B, sharing a railway compartment, each trying to ignore the other.

The Caine Mutiny Court-Martial

ADAPTED FROM Herman Wouk's bestselling novel *The Caine Mutiny*, the play also was written by Wouk. It tells of a fictitious incident during World War II when a junior officer summarily takes the captain of a navy minesweeper off command of his ship. Lieutenant Stephen Maryk (John Hodiak) is court-martialed for his act against Lieutenant Commander Philip Francis Queeg (Lloyd Nolan) and is defended by Lieutenant Barney Greenwald (Henry Fonda). Greenwald is not sympathetic toward Maryk because he believes that Queeg and others who make the Navy their lives are always at the forefront of national defense. Although during the trial he succeeds in breaking down Queeg psychologically and proving that Maryk acted correctly in relieving the captain of his command, he is not happy about the outcome. Darby succeeded in capturing the intensity of the courtroom that was mirrored in the faces of the actors. *The Caine Mutiny Court-Martial*, directed by Charles Laughton and produced by Paul Gregory, opened on January 20, 1954, at the Imperial Theatre.

ABOVE: Lt. Maryk (John Hodiak) being sworn in to testify.

BELOW: Capt. Queeg (Lloyd Nolan) interrogated by Greenwald (Henry Fonda) as the President of the Court (Russell Hicks) looks on.

AGATHA CHRISTIE's mystery thriller did not disappoint Broadway audiences. It takes place in an English courtroom during a murder trial. The key witness, Romaine Heilger-Vole (Patricia Jessel), is the wife of the man on trial, Leonard Vole (Gene Lyons), and gives contradictory testimony, which infuriates the lawyer for the defense, Sir Wilford Robarts (played by Francis L. Sullivan). It all leads to an acquittal for Leonard and a surprise resolution. Produced by Gilbert Miller, it was directed by Robert E. Lewis and opened on December 16, 1954.

ABOVE: Darby captured a tense moment when Sir Wilford closely questions Romaine before Mr. Justice Wainwright (Horace Braham).

Witness for the Prosecution

Silk Stockings

COLE PORTER'S *Silk Stockings* (1955) is one of a long list of Broadway musicals inspired by Hollywood movies—in this case, the Ernst Lubitsch movie *Ninotchka,* starring Greta Garbo. The musical bears little resemblance to the movie except for the romance between Ninotchka, a Soviet investigator who is to report on the actions of three Soviet officials who are not doing enough to promote the Communist cause, and Steve Canfield, an American talent scout who must convince a Soviet composer to write the score for a Hollywood version of *War and Peace*.

Silk Stockings found Cole Porter a bit past his prime; it would be his last Broadway musical. The book by George S. Kaufman and Leueen MacGrath was drastically doctored by Abe Burrows, and producer Cy Feuer took over as director after Kaufman decided to leave the show. Although less successful than previous Porter shows, *Silk Stockings* still ran an impressive 478 performances.

FAR LEFT: Ninotchka (Hildegarde Neff) leaves Paris after being summoned home.

LEFT: Steve (Don Ameche) meets Ninotchka (Neff) and the three Soviet representatives, Ivanov, Brankov, and Bibinski (Henry Lascoe, Leon Belasco, and David Opatoshu).

BELOW: The Russians celebrate Ninotchka's return in the exuberant dance number "The Red Blues."

BELOW: Steve Canfield (Ameche) and Ninotchka (Neff) discovering that they are in love.

RIGHT: Commissar Markovitch (George Tobias) seems more interested in the ballerina (Julie Newmar) than he is in his telephone call.

The Ski...

EILEEN DARBY had many opportunities for great pictures in the production of Thornton Wilder's play *The Skin of Our Teeth,* beginning with the colorful cast that included Tallulah Bankhead, Fredric March, Florence Eldridge, Florence Reed, and Montgomery Clift. The play was part circus, part serious drama, and all of it fun—but with a serious message. Wilder depicted mankind as muddled and befuddled, but manages to survive natural and man-made disasters by the skin of its teeth. The play ranges over 5,000 years, and the principals

change their roles in every age without shedding their symbolic identities. It took a daring producer named Michael Myerberg to present Wilder's play and an imaginative director named Elia Kazan to stage it. The play opened November 18, 1942, when the world was plunged again into war.

LEFT: Montgomery Clift in the uniform of the World War I doughboy. He bears the mark of Cain on his forehead and represents the warrior in every war in every age.

ABOVE: Mr. Antrobus (Fredric March) and his wife (Florence Eldridge) with their children, Gladys (Frances Heflin) and Henry (Clift), as the eternal family that must survive every catastrophe to carry on the human race.

TOP RIGHT: Mrs. Antrobus and Gladys with her baby emerging from the trap door when the "war" is finally over.

RIGHT: Tallulah Bankhead as Sabina, the female life force, who appears in various scenes as the Antrobus maid, Miss Atlantic City, and a wartime camp follower.

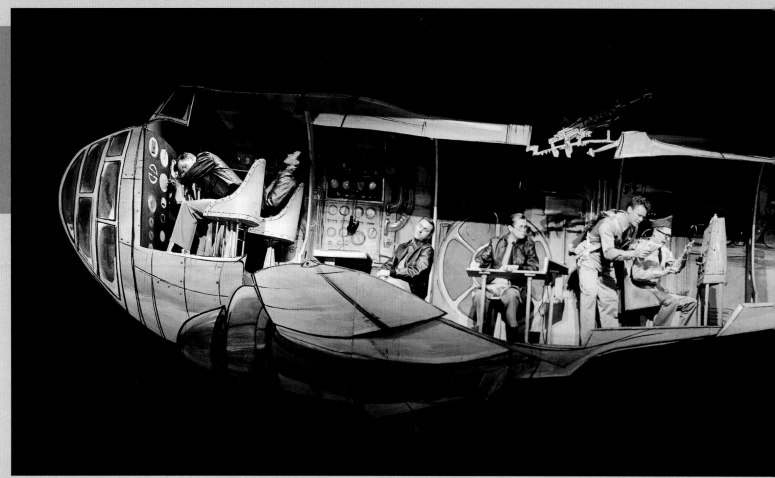

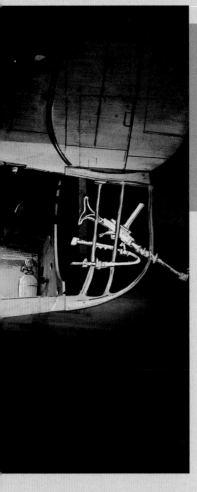

No Time for Sergeants

In 1955 Andy Griffith's career was launched on Broadway after he starred in *No Time for Sergeants* but continued with enormous success in just about all the entertainment media. He would become a household name playing largely the same role in movies and on television: the country hayseed, naïve bumpkin, and irrepressible, plain-talking southern boy. Don Knotts, whose career also began with Ira Levin's play, stayed with the same character as Griffith's perennial sidekick.

The play, about draftees in no particular postwar period, bore little relationship to reality, but audiences loved the

high jinks and wanted to believe that life in the military was not all grim. The play ran so long on Broadway that many of the original actors began moving into different roles as each left for other opportunities.

OPPOSITE TOP: The scene within the airplane reached new heights in hilarity and was a tribute to set designer Peter Larkin.

BOTTOM: Andy Griffith as Will Stockdale with Myron McCormick as Sergeant King.

ABOVE: The original cast included (*left to right*) James Milhollin, Roddy McDowall, Don Knotts, and Robert Webber.

The Desk Set

This 1955 William Marchant comedy seemed to be prescient of the coming of a new electronic era. Into the revered research department of a television network walks a strange man who unnerves head researcher Bunny Watson by snooping in her office and questioning her assistants, all of whom are walking encyclopedias. The man turns out to be an

electronics expert who is sent by the network chief to install a giant computer that will make them all obsolete. Bunny fears for her job and those of her loyal staff, but all ends well when she and the electronics expert fall for each other and the great computer falls apart.

ABOVE: Bunny Watson (Shirley Booth) as the head walking encyclopedia.

The

In 1955, the prestigious Theatre Guild teamed with fledgling producer David Merrick to produce Thornton Wilder's reworking of his 1938 play *The Merchant of Yonkers*. The matchmaker, Dolly Levi, disingenuously promises to arrange a marriage for Horace Vandergelder but really intends to snare him for herself. Meanwhile, Vandergelder's clerks, Cornelius Hackl and Barnaby Tucker, play hooky from their jobs to "have a good meal, live dangerously, nearly get arrested, spend all their money, and not come back to Yonkers until they've kissed a girl."

LEFT: Barnaby (Robert Morse) fulfilling part of his pledge by kissing Mrs. Malloy (Eileen Herlie).

BELOW: Dolly (Ruth Gordon) entertaining Vandergelder (Loring Smith).

Matchmaker

Li'l Abner

In 1956 Norman Panama and Melvin Frank mined
the possibilities of Al Capp's *Li'l Abner* comic strip
and came up with a lively musical, made even
livelier by Michael Kidd's choreography and Johnny
Mercer and Gene de Paul's songs. Set in Dogpatch,
somewhere in the South, the show, with all of the
familiar characters from the strip, derides governmental
inefficiency, corruption, militarists, and politicians.
Along with its strong messages is the comic plot
involving Daisy Mae's never-ending chase to bring
Li'l Abner to the altar, with Marryin' Sam standing
by to do the honors.

FAR LEFT: Marryin' Sam (Stubby Kaye) and friend.

ABOVE: The full cast, including the ever-present
animals, (*left to right*) Marryin' Sam (Stubby Kaye),
Earthquake McGoon (Bern Hoffman), Li'l Abner
(Peter Palmer), Daisy Mae (Edie Adams), and Mammy
and Pappy Yokum (Charlotte Rae and Joe E. Marks).

LEFT: Stupefyin' Jones (Julie Newmar).

Janus

BILLED AS a romantic comedy, Carolyn Green's 1955 play *Janus* was actually an Americanized French farce. It involves two married couples; a member of each carries on a two-month-long affair in New York. Of course, they are discovered, and there is a good deal of comic commotion following the discovery. Add a man from the Internal Revenue Service and the action becomes even more hilariously complicated. The part of the cheating wife was originated by Margaret Sullavan; when she left the cast, her part was taken over by Imogene Coca.

LEFT: The adulterous couple, Jessica (Imogen Coca) and Gil (Robert Preston).

Bells Are Ringing

After Judy Holliday's triumph in *Born Yesterday* in 1951 and a few years in Hollywood, she scored another hit in 1956 with *Bells Are Ringing*. Judy plays Ella Peterson, an operator for Susanswerphone, a telephone message service. Going against the rules, Ella gets involved in the life of one of her clients, a playwright with writer's block named Jeff Moss. Since this is a musical, Ella and Jeff sing and dance their way into each other's lives and hearts.

ABOVE: Ella (Judy Holliday) and Sue (Jean Stapleton), the proprietress of Susanswerphone, at their telephone switchboard.

163

Hello, *Dolly!*

WRITER MICHAEL STEWART recycled Thornton Wilder's play *The Matchmaker* that had served Ruth Gordon so well in 1955 and transformed it into the 1964 musical *Hello, Dolly!* that served Carol Channing even better. With music and lyrics by Jerry Herman, the show was directed and choreographed by Gower Champion and produced by David Merrick. Although he had misgivings, the *New York Times* critic Howard Taubman concluded his review with the words: "Let us rejoice in the blessings *Hello, Dolly!* bestows." After extensive tours, Channing returned to Broadway with the show in 1978 and 1995. She was succeeded in the role by everyone from Ethel Merman (who had originally turned down the part) to Pearl Bailey with an all-black cast in 1974, but it was Channing's performance that was the benchmark for all of the actresses who followed her.

LEFT: Dolly (Channing) hugging her favorite object, Vandergelder's cash register.

RIGHT TOP: Dolly and Horace Vandergelder (David Burns) sealing their engagement with a kiss; CENTER: Cornelius (Charles Nelson Reilly) and Barnaby (Jerry Dodge) plotting their escape from Vandergelder's store; BOTTOM: Mrs. Molloy (Eileen Brennan) singing "Ribbons Down My Back."

AN UNLIKELY MIXTURE of religious persecution, poverty, and the loss of traditions in the Russian village of Anatevka in 1905 was the basis of a show that stunned Broadway in 1964 and has become one of the most beloved musicals of all time. Adapted from Sholom Aleichem's stories, it was a triumph for its creators, Jerry Bock (music), Sheldon Harnick (lyrics), Joseph Stein (book), Jerome Robbins (director-choreographer), and Harold Prince (producer). The cast, led by Zero Mostel as Tevye the dairyman and Maria Karnilova as his wife, Golde, was perfect in every respect. Tevye's struggle for existence in a harsh world and his difficulty in providing for his family and seeing that his daughters are married advantageously struck a responsive chord in the audiences worldwide.

ABOVE: Tevye (Mostel) at the opening of the show. Boris Aronson's scenery of the impoverished Anatevka and Tevye's humble abode was so true that it became part of the seamless whole of the production.

RIGHT: Tevye (Mostel) explains a dream to Golde (Karnilova), which evoked the deceased Grandma Tzeitel (Sue Babel) to justify his daughter Tzeitel's wish to marry the poor tailor Motel (Austin Pendleton).

TOP RIGHT: Tzeitel and Motel's wedding dance.

Fiddler on the Roof

LEFT: Darby captured the many moods of Mostel in a series of pictures of his mobile face.

BELOW: Mostel and Karnilova in rehearsal with director Jerome Robbins.

NEAR RIGHT: A bit of levity between Mostel and Karnilova during rehearsal.

FAR RIGHT: Eileen Darby backstage with Mostel. Darby once said: "You had to watch out for Zero Mostel. He had all the chorus girls in *Fiddler* running behind the scenery every time the curtain fell so

that they could avoid getting their bottoms pinched. He lunged at me once but didn't catch me."

Although Mostel made Tevye his signature role and played it for many years both on Broadway and on tours, the strength of the musical allowed many others to follow him in the role, including Luther Adler, Herschel Bernardi, Harry Goz, Jerry Jarrett, Paul Lipson, Jan Peerce, and, in 1971, Topol, who starred in the screen version.

CHARACTER *Portraits*

LEFT: GREGORY PECK (1916–2003) as CHRISTY MAHON in *The Playboy of the Western World*, 1946. Eileen Darby traveled to a summer theater on Cape Cod to photograph Peck in this modern Irish classic. Although the play never made it to Broadway with Peck as the star, it has been revived many times.

RIGHT: SPENCER TRACY (1900–1967) as MOREY VINION in *The Rugged Path*, 1945. Tracy had been away from the Broadway stage for fifteen years when he was prevailed upon by Katharine Hepburn to star in this play by Robert Sherwood, which was tailor-made for him. Although Tracy received glowing notices for his portrayal of a high-minded newspaper editor, he returned to Hollywood after only a ten-week run.

LEFT: JUDITH ANDERSON (1898–1992) as LADY MACBETH, 1941. Rarely has an actress playing this role received the plaudits that Judith Anderson did. Most thought it was the greatest performance of the time. The *New York Times* critic thought her sleepwalking scene was "too frightful to be watched"; another critic considered the scene "a masterpiece of invention and suspense."

RIGHT (*right to left*):
KATHARINE CORNELL (1898–1974) as MASHA, JUDITH ANDERSON (1898–1992) as OLGA, and GERTRUDE MUSGROVE (b. 1912) as IRINA in *Three Sisters,* 1942. The actresses gave new luster to their roles in this revival of Chekhov's play. Rarely have such massive talents blended so well on the Broadway stage. Cornell and Anderson both had enviable stage careers, excelling in a wide range of roles from classic to contemporary.

BELOW: REX HARRISON (1908–1990) as HENRY VIII in *Anne of the Thousand Days,* 1948. Although English-born Harrison made brief appearances on Broadway in the 1930s, it was this role in Maxwell Anderson's play that launched his career in America. Harrison's Broadway career hit its zenith with his unforgettable performance in *My Fair Lady* (1956). He won Tony Awards for both.

LEFT: BORIS KARLOFF (1887–1969) as CAPTAIN HOOK in *Peter Pan,* 1950. Despite a distinguished career on the stage in London and New York, Karloff is mostly remembered for his role as the Monster in the movie *Frankenstein.* In addition to *Peter Pan,* Karloff appeared on Broadway in *Arsenic and Old Lace* (1941), *The Linden Tree* (1948), and *The Lark* (1955).

LEFT: MONTGOMERY CLIFT (1920–1966) in *Foxhole in the Parlor,* 1945. The brooding, contemplative mood of Montgomery Clift suited the roles he was to play in many plays and movies almost from the beginning of his career on Broadway and in Hollywood. Here he is cast as a young artist home from the war and suffering its searing consequences.

RIGHT: RUBY DEE (b. 1924) and OSSIE DAVIS (b. 1917) in *Jeb,* 1946. The civil rights movement began (at least on Broadway) immediately after the end of World War I. The play *Jeb* by Robert Ardrey was not a success, although its message of the evils of discrimination was echoed many times in the years to come. It marked the Broadway debut of one of the most enduring and respected husband-wife teams in the theater's history.

LEFT: PATRICIA NEAL (b. 1926) as REGINA HUBBARD in *Another Part of the Forest*, 1947. The actress gave a Tony Award–winning performance in Lillian Hellman's play, which introduced audiences to the Hubbard family twenty years before they appeared in Hellman's *The Little Foxes*. Neal eventually was lured to Hollywood, where her career flourished.

RIGHT: HELEN HAYES (1900–1993) as HARRIET BEECHER STOWE in *Harriet*, 1944. After an absence of two years, Helen Hayes returned to Broadway in a role that fit her like a glove. *Harriet* tells the story of a disinterested citizen who becomes a fierce abolitionist and writes *Uncle Tom's Cabin*. Hayes never disappointed her audiences nor, for that matter, the critics.

LEFT: WALTER MATTHAU (1920–2000) as CHARLIE HILL in *In Any Language* (1952). Matthau had to wait until 1965 to find the role that would define his professional career for the rest of his life: Oscar Madison in *The Odd Couple*. Until that point, he appeared in a dozen or so plays on Broadway; some were moderate successes, others, flops. Count this production among the latter.

ABOVE: MARY ASTOR (1906–1987) in *Many Happy Returns*. Primarily known as a movie star, Mary Astor appeared on Broadway from time to time. In 1945 she starred in this mangled version of a Claire Kummer comedy. It was a resounding flop and Astor retreated to Hollywood.

BELOW: DAME MAY WHITTY (1865–1948) as MADAME RAQUIN in *Therese*, 1945. May Whitty made her first stage appearance in London in 1881 and her last appearance on Broadway in this production. She was eighty years old when she took this role and stole the show from its stars. In 1918, she was made Dame Commander of the British Empire for her charitable work during World War I.

RIGHT: EDWARD EVERETT HORTON (1886–1970) as HENRY DEWLIP in *Springtime for Henry* was the darling of the summer theater circuit for more than twenty years, playing this fussy, rich playboy. He first revived it for Broadway in 1951, where it failed to convulse audiences or critics, so Horton took it back on the road.

BEHIND THE *Scenes*

LEFT: ELIA KAZAN (*director*), 1944. Kazan's directorial method was mostly physical, not intellectual—often a gesture would be enough to convey what he wanted. Here he is in action during a rehearsal for *Jacobowsky and the Colonel*, a play by S. N. Behrman, which starred Annabella and Louis Calhern.

RIGHT: LEONARD BERNSTEIN (*composer*) and JEROME ROBBINS (*choreographer*), 1944. The musical *On the Town* opened to rave reviews and became a benchmark in the history of the genre, largely because of the efforts of its extraordinary creative team. Here two members of that team watch a rehearsal of the show.

ABOVE LEFT: GEORGE S. KAUFMAN (*director*), 1946. No one on Broadway had a sharper wit than George S. Kaufman, who was a sought-after director and play doctor. He enjoyed enormous success with his partners, collaborating with such talented cowriters as Moss Hart, Marc Connelly, Edna Ferber, and Howard Teichman. He is shown here at a rehearsal of *Miss Liberty*.

CENTER (*left to right*): HENRY and PHOEBE EPHRON (*writers*), GEORGE ABBOTT (*director*), and HAROLD PRINCE (*producer*) attending auditions for *Take Her, She's Mine* (1961). Their choices for this lightweight comedy were Elizabeth Ashley, Art Carney, Phyllis Thaxter, and June Harding.

RIGHT: IRVING BERLIN (*composer*), 1949. Very few have contributed more to the American musical form than Irving Berlin. His musicals, including *This Is the Army* (1942), *Annie Get Your Gun* (1946), *Miss Liberty* (1949), and *Call Me Madam* (1950) have become the new classics of the theater. He is shown here at a rehearsal of *Miss Liberty*.

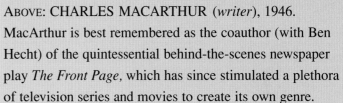

ABOVE: CHARLES MACARTHUR (*writer*), 1946. MacArthur is best remembered as the coauthor (with Ben Hecht) of the quintessential behind-the-scenes newspaper play *The Front Page,* which has since stimulated a plethora of television series and movies to create its own genre.

LEFT: COLE PORTER (*composer*), 1944. Undoubtedly, Porter (*left*) intended his wartime musical *Mexican Hayride* to be unapologetically escapist. HASSARD SHORT (*center*) directed and MIKE TODD (*right*) produced this bit of fun, but it was the great comedian Bobby Clark who kept all the nonsense together.

BELOW LEFT: ROBERT E. SHERWOOD (*writer*), 1940. For more than two decades, Robert E. Sherwood was one of the most prolific playwrights on the American stage. His antiwar drama *There Shall Be No Night* was photographed by Eileen Darby early in her career. He is shown (*left*) with RICHARD WHORF, who served as costume designer for the production.

LEFT: JACK COLE (*choreographer*), 1947. One of Broadway's legendary pioneering choreographers, Cole danced along with his dancers when he rehearsed them. Among his many credits are *Kismet*, *A Funny Thing Happened on the Way to the Forum*, and *Man of La Mancha*. Working with him is the rehearsal pianist, a necessary adjunct to every musical production.

ABOVE: ROBERT RUSSELL BENNETT (*arranger*), 1945. Every notable composer on Broadway, including Richard Rodgers, Fritz Loewe, Irving Berlin, Jerome Kern, Cole Porter, Arthur Schwartz, and George Gershwin, sooner or later called upon Bennett to orchestrate their works. He was Broadway's indispensable man, with dozens of scores to his credit.

OPPOSITE: LILLIAN HELLMAN (*writer*), c. 1940. "I had heard about how difficult Lillian Hellman could be and about her tart tongue, but I never saw any of it," Darby recalled. "She was a pussy cat with me, both at her home in Westchester and her apartment in New York, where she allowed me to photograph her. Every time I met up with her in the future, she never failed to greet me like a friend."

ABOVE: CLARE BOOTHE LUCE (*writer*), c. 1935. Not only was she Mrs. Henry Luce, the wife of the boss at *Life*, she was a Broadway playwright; a war correspondent; a congresswoman from Connecticut; and an ambassador to Italy.

ABOVE: ANITA LOOS (*writer*), 1946. The perpetual flapper, Loos wore her 1920s hairstyle for the rest of her life. She is most famous for penning *Gentlemen Prefer Blondes,* which first appeared on stage in 1926; in 1949, Carol Channing made the role of Lorelei Lee her own, followed by Marilyn Monroe in the film version.

ABOVE: IRENE SELZNICK and
TENNESSEE WILLIAMS (*writer*), 1947.
Selznick (*left*) was a first-time producer when
she hit the jackpot with *Streetcar*. After the
Broadway opening in December 1947, a
road company was quickly assembled and
dispatched to tour the country. Here,
Selznick and Williams take a break with
the stars of the road tour, Anthony Quinn
(as Stanley) and Uta Hagen (as Blanche).

JOAN OF LORRAINE, 1946.
"I was really looking forward to photographing Ingrid Bergman in *Joan of Lorraine*," Darby remembered. "I had never photographed her and I was delighted to be called to shoot the rehearsal and the show in Washington, D.C., where it would be trying out before arriving on Broadway. Unfortunately, I started to get the sniffles while I was photographing the

rehearsal and I knew that by the time I had to go to Washington, it would be a full-blown cold which I could have passed on to her. So I had to give up the assignment to someone else. It was a big disappointment, but I was able, at least, to do the rehearsal." *Clockwise from top left:* Costars Sam Wanamaker and Ingrid Bergman; playwright Maxwell Anderson; and Bergman and director Margo Jones.

ABOVE: MICHAEL TODD (*producer*), 1943. Without the cigar in his mouth, Todd would have been unrecognizable. A showman in the old Broadway tradition, he had a string of successes ranging from *The Hot Mikado* (1939) to Maurice Evans's *Hamlet* (1946). Here he presides over a rehearsal for the Cole Porter musical *Something for the Boys.*

RIGHT: RICHARD RODGERS (*composer*), 1943. "During the dress rehearsal for *Oklahoma!*, there was a lot of waiting around while things were getting fixed," Darby remembered. "Rodgers was sitting in the auditorium and looked bored. He picked up a chorus girl's hat, plopped it on his head, and lit up a cigar. This was too good a picture to pass up and I photographed him. But it never got published at the time I took it because his wife, Dorothy, thought it was undignified."

ABOVE: RICHARD RODGERS (*composer*) and OSCAR HAMMERSTEIN II (*lyricist*), 1943. After Hart's death, Rodgers found an ideal partner in Oscar Hammerstein II, and together they rewrote the history of the American musical. They are shown here conferring during a rehearsal of their first collaboration, *Oklahoma!*, which would open down the street from *A Connecticut Yankee*.

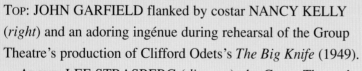

TOP: JOHN GARFIELD flanked by costar NANCY KELLY (*right*) and an adoring ingénue during rehearsal of the Group Theatre's production of Clifford Odets's *The Big Knife* (1949).

ABOVE: LEE STRASBERG (*director*), the Group Theatre's guru, directing Nancy Kelly in *The Big Knife*. Strasberg founded the Actors Studio and taught what is known today as the Method school of acting.

LEFT: GRACE KELLY in Strindberg's *The Father* (1949), her debut on Broadway. RAYMOND MASSEY was both star and director of the play.

BELOW (*left to right*): Producer BILLY ROSE, lyricist OSCAR HAMMERSTEIN, director HASSARD SHORT, and other members of the production team at a rehearsal of *Carmen Jones* (1943), Hammerstein's contemporary re-creation of Bizet's opera, with an all-black cast.

ABOVE: JED HARRIS (*director*), 1942. Harris quit Yale in his senior year to become Broadway's *enfant terrible*. His brilliance as a director was undeniable, but his abrasive personality and monumental ego alienated most of his collaborators, and his longtime love affair with Ruth Gordon was the talk of Broadway for many years.

ABOVE: MOSS HART (*writer*), c. 1946. Playwright Moss Hart found a soul mate and collaborator in George S. Kaufman with whom he wrote seven plays, all of which were hits and one of which (*You Can't Take It with You*) won the Pulitzer Prize. Hart often directed his own plays, but his greatest directorial triumph was Lerner and Loewe's *My Fair Lady*.

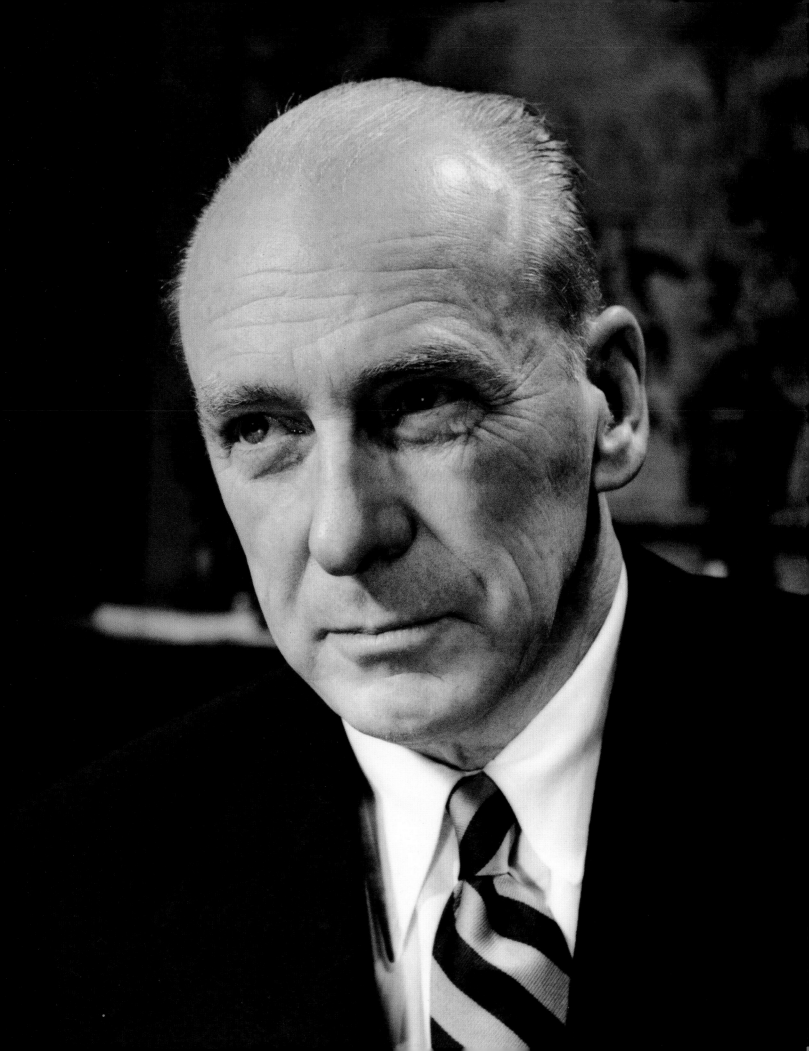

Epilogue

"No one gets out of life alive," said Tennessee Williams, one of Eileen Darby's most memorable subjects. On March 30, 2004, after suffering a fall and surgery that left her unable to speak, Darby herself departed the world to which she bore sensational witness. Up until her fall, she had bustled through life with the vigor and curiosity that informed her photographs. The defining pictures she left behind are both her history and the exuberant history of theatrical times gone by. They record a world of joy and passion and high jinks, which was also Darby's oxygen. Her photographs are part of the nation's collective memory; no book about postwar Broadway can be written without their presence and the enduring brand of "Graphic House. Photograph by Eileen Darby."

RIGHT: *Eileen Darby explains the setup of her next shot to Bea Lillie and the cast of* Inside U.S.A. *(1948).*

202

A SELECTED PORTFOLIO OF SHOWS

~

Eileen Darby photographed more than six hundred Broadway shows in her lifetime. The following selection illustrates the diversity of her work, from the unremarkable to the classic plays and musicals of the Broadway stage. Her portrait work of some of the greats of the stage is also listed.

Bravo!
Edward, My Son
Goodbye, My Fancy
The Hallams
Heaven on Earth
Hold It!
Joy to the World
Kathleen
Kiss Me, Kate
Last Dance
The Leading Lady
Lend an Ear
The Linden Tree
Look, Ma, I'm Dancin'!
Macbeth
The Madwoman of Chaillot
The Rape of Lucretia
Red Gloves
Rosario and Antonio
Sleepy Hollow
Summer and Smoke
Sundown Beach
Town House
Where's Charley?

1949
All for Love
Along Fifth Avenue
The Big Knife
The Biggest Thief in Town
The Browning Version
Caesar and Cleopatra *R*
Clutterbuck
Death of a Salesman
The Father *R*
Gentlemen Prefer Blondes
Harlequinade
King Richard III *R*
The Man Who Came to Dinner
Miss Liberty
Montserrat
Mrs. Gibbon's Boys
Regina
South Pacific
Texas, L'il Darlin'
That Lady
Touch and Go
Yes, M'Lord

1950
Affairs of State
Alive and Kicking
As You Like It *R*
The Barrier
Bless You All
Call Me Madam
The Cocktail Party
The Consul
Cry of the Peacock
The Day After Tomorrow
The Enchanted
Great to Be Alive!
Guys and Dolls
Happy as Larry
Hilda Crane
Legend of Sarah

The Liar
The Member of the Wedding
Out of This World
Pardon Our French
Peter Pan *R*
Tickets, Please!
The Wisteria Trees

1951
Angel in the Pawnshop
The Autumn Garden
Don Juan in Hell
Gigi
Gramercy Ghost
Seventeen
The Small Hours
Springtime for Henry *R*
A Tree Grows in Brooklyn
Two on the Aisle

1952
The Children's Hour *R*
Dial M for Murder
An Evening with Beatrice Lillie
The Grey-Eyed People
In Any Language
The Long Watch
My Darlin' Aida
Of Thee I Sing *R*
Pal Joey *R*
Three Wishes for Jamie
Two's Company

1953
The Bat *R*
Be Your Age
Can-Can
Carnival in Flanders
Cyrano de Bergerac *R*
Dead Pigeon
A Girl Can Tell
Hazel Flagg
In the Summer House
John Brown's Body
John Murray Anderson's
    Almanac
Late Love
Me and Juliet
On Borrowed Time *R*
A Pin to See the Peep Show
Room Service *R*
Sabrina Fair
The Solid Gold Cadillac
The Teahouse of the August
    Moon
The Trip to Bountiful

1954
Anniversary Waltz
Burning Glass
The Caine Mutiny Court-Martial
Dear Charles
The Living Room
Lunatics and Lovers
Mademoiselle Colombe
The Magic and the Loss

One Eye Closed
Portrait of a Lady
Reclining Figure
The Tender Trap
Witness for the Prosecution

1955
Cat on a Hot Tin Roof
The Dark Is Light Enough
Deadfall
The Desk Set
Janus
The Matchmaker
A Month in the Country *R*
No Time for Sergeants
A Roomful of Roses
Silk Stockings
The Southwest Corner
Young and Beautiful

1956
Bells Are Ringing
The Great Sebastians
Happy Hunting
King John
Li'l Abner
The Littlest Revue
Too Late the Phalarope
Ziegfeld Follies of 1956

1957
The First Gentleman
West Side Story

1964
Fiddler on the Roof
Hello, Dolly!

PERSONALITY PORTRAITS
Anita Alvarez
Don Ameche
Louis Armstrong
Desi Arnaz and Lucille Ball
Sono Asato
W. H. Auden
Leonard Bernstein
Jan Clayton
Montgomery Clift and
    Marlene Dietrich
Imogene Coca
Alexander Cohen
Henri Christophe
Howard Cullman
B. Field and E. Rice
Peggy Ann Garner
Ruth Gordon
June Havoc
Helen Hayes
Peter Lind Hayes
Scott Hazel
Willy Howard
Garson Kanin and Ruth Gordon
Serge Koussevitsky
Beatrice Lillie
Anita Loos
Bambi Lynn

Thomas Mann
Mary Martin
Joan McCracken
Zero Mostel
Charles Muench
Edith Piaf
Vincent Price
Louis Prima
Roy Rogers
Jimmy Savo
Jack Teagarden
Charles Trenet
Orson Welles
Tennessee Williams

UNDATED WORK
Admirable Bashville
Between Covers
Big People
Bizarre Bazaar
Bonanza Bound
Bruno and Sidney
By Appointment Only
Captain Carvallo
The Clover Ring
Courting Time
Dancing in the Streets
Dark Memory
Darkout Hour
Dinner for Three
Emerald Staircase
Glad to See You
Heartsong
House on the Cliff
Income Tax
Johnny Kissed Me
Marching with Johnny
Miss Jones
Much Ado About Love
Of All People
Office Manners
Old Man Devil
One Shoe off
Opening Nights
The Peacemaker
Portrait of Happiness
Ring Around the Moon
Sands of the Negev
Son and I
Sons of Fun
Spring in Brazil
Stardust
Strivers Row
Storm Operations
Stove Pipe Hat
Tally Ho
Tars and Spars
That's the Ticket
Theatre Inc.
There's Always Juliet
Tin Top Valley
Twilight Bar

R = Revival

Index

ABOVE: *A holiday card drawn for Eileen Darby by her friend of sixty years, Al Hirschfeld, c. 1944.*

MERRY CHRISTMAS • EILEEN DARBY

RIGHT: *An avid theatergoer, First Lady Eleanor Roosevelt is seen exiting a Broadway theater via the stage door with escort Mayor Fiorello LaGuardia, c. 1942.*

Photo Credits

All images © Eileen Darby with the exception of the following: Museum of the City of New York: 83 bottom, 99, 101 bottom, 154; Billy Rose Theatre Collection, The New York Public Library for the Performing Arts, Astor, Lenox and Tilden Foundations: 82–83, 100 left, 124 all, 124–25, 127.